CHILDREN'S LITERATURE & SOCIAL STUDIES

Selecting and Using Notable Books in the Classroom

EDITED BY

MYRA ZARNOWSKI AND ARLENE F. GALLAGHER

KENDALL/HUNT PUBLISHING COMPANY
4050 Westmark Drive   Dubuque, Iowa 52002

National Council for the Social Studies

Editorial staff on this publication: Salvatore J. Natoli, Pamela D. Hollar, M. Angela Olson
Cover design: Paul Wolski   Publication design: Dan Kaufman

Library of Congress Catalog Card Number: 93-79688
ISBN 0-8403-8951-5

Table of Contents

This book is dedicated to the memory of John Donovan, who served for many years as Executive Director of the Children's Book Council Review Board, and to Arlene Gallagher, coeditor and contributor to this volume, who died shortly before its publication. This was a project she valued as part of her overall commitment to acquaint teachers and children with books addressing social issues. Arlene's enthusiasm for children's literature and social studies enriched the lives of the members of the National Council for the Social Studies-Children's Book Council Joint Committee.

Grateful appreciation is extended to the following people who reviewed all of the manuscripts and offered many helpful suggestions:

Ruth Cline, Past President of the National Council of Teachers of English and Professor of Education at the University of Colorado in Boulder.

Mary McFarland, Past President of National Council for the Social Studies, and Instructional Coordinator of Social Studies K–12 and Director of Staff Development in the Parkway School District, Saint Louis County, Missouri.

Matilda Welter, Senior Editor of Children's Trade Books at the Houghton Mifflin Company in Boston, Massachusetts.

Contributors

All of the contributors are either present or former members of the Book Review Subcommittee of the National Council for the Social Studies-Children's Book Council Joint Committee.

Jacqueline A. Abbott is Professor of Education at Eastern Connecticut State University in Willimantic, specializing in children's literature and social studies curriculum. She was an elementary school classroom teacher for thirteen years.

Jane Brem has taught kindergarten through graduate school and has worked with various museum education programs. She presently coordinates field experiences for students in the Master in Teaching program at Seattle University in Seattle, Washington.

Arlene F. Gallagher was Professor Emerita at Elms College, Chicopee, Massachusetts. She taught courses and institutes in children's literature and social studies and was the editor for "Children's Literature and Social Studies" for *Social Studies and the Young Learner*.

Alvis T. Harthern chairs the Early Childhood Education Department at West Georgia College in Carrollton. She teaches undergraduate and graduate social studies methods courses as well as a graduate literacy course.

Cherryl Sage is a library and media specialist in Anne Arundel County, Maryland. She has developed numerous conference presentations, journal articles, and curriculum materials on the topic of using literature to teach social studies.

Robert Stremme is an elementary school teacher in the Centennial School District in Pennsylvania. He is also an education instructor at Eastern College in Saint David's, Pennsylvania.

Vickie Weiss teaches a combined 4th and 5th grade at Indian Hill School in Grand Blanc, Michigan. She attended the National Geographic Society Summer Geography Institute in 1990, which renewed her "geographic spirit."

Shirley Wilton teaches children's literature at Ocean County College in Toms River, New Jersey. She holds degrees from Connecticut College in New London and the University of Michigan in Ann Arbor.

Christina B. Woll is former coordinator of library services for the El Paso, Texas, public schools. She now works as a consultant/reviewer and is a department editor for *Social Studies and the Young Learner*.

Judith S. Wooster currently works with children, teachers, and books in Three Village Central School District in Long Island, New York. She has taught elementary students, and directed curriculum and instruction for the Bureau of Social Studies of the New York State Education Department and the Stanford Program on International and Cross-Cultural Education at Stanford University.

Myra Zarnowski is Associate Professor of Elementary and Early Childhood Education at Queens College in Flushing, New York, where she teaches courses in children's literature, social studies, and language arts.

Jack Zevin, Professor of Education at Queens College in Flushing, New York, is author of *Social Studies for the Twenty-First Century* and contributing editor to *The Social Studies* and *Social Science Record*.

Foreword

In the late 1960s, social studies teachers, under the auspices of National Council for the Social Studies, began meeting the children's book publisher members of the Children's Book Council to discuss common interests. These early discussions suggested the value of a permanent liaison committee. The resultant NCSS-CBC Joint Committee, established in 1971, focused its attention on developing ways to present up-to-date information about children's trade books within a framework meaningful to social studies teachers.

Since 1971, a subcommittee of social studies educators has assembled, with the administrative help of the Children's Book Council, an annual list of Notable Children's Trade Books in the Field of Social Studies. The list appears initially in a spring issue of the NCSS journal, *Social Education,* and is subsequently reprinted by CBC and broadly distributed throughout the United States.

As an extension of this bibliographic work, the committee prepares programs, articles, and publications aimed toward helping elementary and middle school social studies teachers develop strategies for using trade books effectively in the classroom. It is the committee's belief that trade books should be an important component of the materials available to children in grades K–8.

In addition to this cooperative work with NCSS, the Children's Book Council engages in joint activities with other national organizations, most notably the American Booksellers Association, the American Library Association, the International Reading Association, the National Council of Teachers of English, and the National Science Teachers Association. In each case, the Children's Book Council's work is intended to encourage young people to read and enjoy books, and to promote an educated citizenry for whom reading is a lifelong activity.

The National Council for the Social Studies-Children's Book Council Joint Committee welcomes ideas from readers of this volume for projects the Joint Committee might undertake that would help educators and children's trade book publishers reach children with the excitement of learning and literature. Please share your thoughts by writing to the following addresses:

The Children's Book Council
568 Broadway, Suite 404
New York, NY 10012

National Council for the Social Studies
3501 Newark Street, NW
Washington, DC 20016

David Riederman
The Children's Book Council

Introduction

As members of the National Council for the Social Studies-Children's Book Council Joint Committee, we have had the opportunity to read hundreds of trade books and select those we think will best serve the needs of social studies teachers and students. It has been truly one of the best jobs we ever had.

Committee members, appointed by the NCSS President, come from classrooms, libraries, media centers, and universities all over the country. These ten or twelve people meet once or twice each year at the Children's Book Council headquarters in New York City.

During our committee meetings we would passionately discuss, joke about, argue over, and promote our favorite titles. From these stimulating discussions, the idea for this volume evolved.

This book extends the committee's role of identifying titles for the annual list of Notable Children's Trade Books in the Field of Social Studies so that members, both past and present, can share their ideas for using these titles in the classroom. The result is a practical collection of information and literature-based teaching ideas designed primarily for social studies teachers at the elementary and junior high school levels.

Social studies teachers must be familiar with children's books *and* know how to use them purposefully. As a result, this volume is divided into two parts. Part 1 examines the selection of books for classroom instruction; Part 2 addresses incorporating children's literature into the social studies program.

The authors included in Part 1 discuss the criteria for selecting books and recommend specific titles for classroom use. Christina B. Woll reviews nonfiction books that make good read-aloud choices and shares some useful tips for teachers who want to begin read-aloud programs. Cherryl Sage discusses the criteria for selecting picture books for social studies programs and provides an annotated bibliography for the K–8 classroom. Bob Stremme offers examples of children's books teachers can use to help children understand the five fundamental themes of geography—location, place, human-environment interactions, movement, and regions. He also suggests how these books might be used as a springboard for other geography-related activities. Shirley Wilton examines the features of newer biographies, explains why they are better than ever, and recommends titles for classroom use. Part 1 concludes with Jack Zevin's analysis of young adult books that analyze war and conflict. He provides suggestions for engaging students in critically examining an author's viewpoint. Taken together, the chapters in Part 1 answer, at least in part, a relevant question: What books can be used effectively when teaching social studies?

The authors of Part 2 illustrate the role of trade books in classroom instruction. Chapters 6 through 9 take us directly into classrooms and vividly illustrate the value of reading and talking about books. Arlene F. Gallagher takes us to a talk show featuring characters from the past. She describes how a talk show format can bring to life the drama found in biographies, autobiographies, and historical novels. Myra Zarnowski ushers us into a 6th grade classroom where students read and discuss books about significant social issues— poverty, human rights, immigration, the environment, and civil rights—and then write personal essays with voice and conviction. Vicki Weiss, a classroom teacher, takes us along as she and her students go through the process of adopting a nearby highway exit. This project, which enabled students to learn firsthand about preserving a wetland site, shows the power of a single trade book to stimulate thought and action. Jane Brem shows how trade books can foster learning in a number of ways: directing children's attention to important concepts, serving as models for extensive writing projects, and stimulating interest in a topic. She provides examples of classroom instruction at several grade levels.

Chapters 10 through 12 focus our attention on curriculum planning. Judith S. Wooster explains the process of developing literature packets, collections of literature-based activities that develop key social science ideas. She demonstrates through examples that purposeful planning is the key to this endeavor.

Alvis T. Harthern explains how literature folders—questions and activities based on selected books—are particularly appropriate for children working in cooperative learning groups. In the final essay, Jacqueline A. Abbott provides an example of the focus-unit approach to teaching social studies. Using six biographies from the NCSS-CBC Notable list, she provides a series of lessons that explore the lives of people who took risks.

Taken together, the chapters in Part 2 address the question: How can teachers use children's literature as part of classroom instruction?

Our purpose in compiling these essays is to illustrate the place of children's literature in social studies programs. This is a beginning. We hope it stimulates *more* teachers to introduce *more* literature to *more* children so that social studies becomes a vibrant, challenging, and exciting subject for both teachers and students.

Myra Zarnowski
Arlene F. Gallagher
Editors

Chapter One

Nonfiction Read-Aloud Programs

Christina B. Woll

Like recipes from a family cookbook, successful read-aloud programs have familiar ingredients and simple instructions.

A favorite nonfiction recipe goes something like this:

Social Studies Read-Aloud

1 Part Read-Aloud Know-How

1 Part Reading Interests Savvy

1 Part Top-Flight Children's Books

Combine ingredients carefully, paying particular attention to the quality of books selected. Plan thoroughly. The result will be a memorable, curriculum-reinforcing, read-aloud program for middle grade students.

Jim Trelease, writing in his popular *New Read-Aloud Handbook* (1989), extols the value of reading aloud to children. He comments that such reading stimulates the listener's interest, emotional development, imagination, and language development.

Jim Trelease is correct. Reading aloud pays off in growth of vocabulary and listening skills, knowledge level, and background building. Read-aloud programs in schools across the land attest to the power of this concept.

The materials used in read-aloud programs are most often fiction, but nonfiction resources with lively, well-written texts also have their place. In social studies, such books coupled with strong program design provide solid learning experiences.

Read-Aloud Know-How

Once the desire to develop a read-aloud program is in place, it is time to set the scene with the careful planning that is so important to developing a successful program. Consider these suggestions.

- Set aside a specific read-aloud time on a regular basis three or more times per week. The nature of the material and curriculum intent should help determine the frequency of reading aloud.
- Establish a climate that shows you value reading aloud.

- Select materials you enjoy. If the reader is bored, think how the listeners must feel.
- Realize that it is not necessary to read all books from beginning to end. Reading a small section may be equally effective.
- Read at an easy, moderate pace. Beginners often read too rapidly. Try a practice session with a friend.
- Use a picture or other props if desired. The possibilities are many: food, clothing or period items, maps and globes, or music, for example. Do not allow the props to overwhelm the reading activity, however; less is more.
- Know your materials and select in advance a satisfactory stopping point while promising more to come.
- Indicate to listeners when you will read again and keep to the schedule.
- Allow listeners time to consider and absorb the information presented. Resist the temptation for long, didactic discussions.
- Ask your librarian to help you prepare a list of nonfiction and fiction materials related to the subject of your read-aloud book. Use your read-aloud program as the cornerstone for development of thematic activities.

Reading Interests Savvy

Key in developing an effective nonfiction read-aloud program is an alert awareness of students' interests and characteristics. Keep both interests and developmental characteristics in mind as you select read-aloud titles.

Middle grade students are growing more attentive to the world about them and are developing interest about relationships in that world. At this age, students' abilities to grasp chronological aspects of historical materials have improved markedly. Anecdotal information is popular and adventure stories are long-time favorites as are simple biographies.

In choosing read-alouds, the quality of writing is vital. Vague or generalized material will not hold listeners' attention. Only the strongest, clearest writing works. Quality tells.

Top-Flight Books

Approximately four hundred children's nonfiction library or trade books in social studies are published each year. Some of the new books are interesting but are poorly written; others are written by skilled authors but address subjects that lack appeal. Some of the new books are mediocre or worse. But each year some excellent books are published, and perhaps ten or twenty of the total number are strong read-aloud candidates.

Fortunately for program planners, the qualities that make a good read-aloud (i.e., an intriguing topic and well-written text) also bring recognition and favorable reviews. As a result, good read-alouds find their way into elementary school library media centers and children's rooms of public libraries.

Read-Aloud Winners

U.S. history topics offer many read-aloud possibilities.

Homes in the Wilderness: A Pilgrim's Journal of Plymouth Plantation in 1620 by William Bradford and Others of the Mayflower Company by Margaret Wise Brown (1988) is an adaptation of a work that describes the pilgrims' first winter in North America. It could be used as a winter-long reading project or as a companion volume to two books by Marcia Sewall, *The Pilgrims of Plimoth* (1986) and *People of the Breaking Day* (1990).

Buttons for General Washington by Peter and Connie Roop (1986) is a fictionalized telling of the adventures of 14-year-old John Darragh as he takes messages from British-occupied Philadelphia to General Washington's Valley Forge camp.

In *Sybil Rides for Independence* by Drollene P. Brown (1985), another book with an American Revolution setting, the reader and listener follow young Sybil Luddington as she rides to warn the minutemen of the British attack on Danbury.

Anecdotes abound in Jean Fritz's acclaimed *Shh! We're Writing the Constitution* (1987), a carefully craft-

PEOPLE OF THE BREAKING DAY
written and illustrated by Marcia Sewall

From *People of the Breaking Day*, © 1990 Marcia Sewall, reprinted by permission of Atheneum Publishers, a division of Macmillan Publishing Company.

ed history of the events of the Constitutional Convention. *The Birth of a Nation: The Early Years of the United States* by Doris and Harold Faber (1989) combines solid scholarship and writing ability to provide a vigorous picture of events and individuals involved in the 1787–97 era of U.S. government. Although this title is tough going for young readers, it works well with upper elementary students as a read-aloud.

Albert Marrin, history professor and skilled author, has written several books with notable potential as read-alouds. Two with American history ties are *The War for Independence: The Story of the American Revolution* (1988) and *1812: The War Nobody Won* (1985). The latter is spiced with detailed description of life on a ship; the whole class will react when the section describing sailors' food is read.

The Incredible Journey of Lewis and Clark by Rhoda Blumberg (1987) chronicles the explorers' seven-thousand-mile expedition from Saint Louis to the Pacific Coast. The text is lively and provides a suitable base for expanded study.

The Pioneers Go West by George Stewart (1982) is a reissued title from the familiar Landmark series first published four decades ago. Stewart chronicles the westward journey of a group of pioneers traveling from Ohio to California in the 1840s. Based on fact, the text recreates the difficulties and daily life of the arduous trip.

Shh!
We're Writing
the Constitution
by Jean Fritz

pictures by Tomie dePaola

From *Shh! We're Writing the Constitution,* © 1987 illustrations by Tomie dePaola, reprinted by permission of G. P. Putnam's Sons.

Compiled with excellent documentation by Doreen Rappaport, *Escape from Slavery: Five Journeys to Freedom* (1991) details five pre–Civil War stories of slaves who fled to freedom.

Milton Meltzer's *Voices from the Civil War: A Documentary History of the Great American Conflict* (1989) contains excerpts from interviews, letters, and other writings of the period. Portions of the work are particularly meaningful when used as a read-aloud during study of the Civil War.

In the recent Newbery Award–winner *Buffalo Hunt* by Russell Freedman (1988), vivid text meshed with detail describes the many ways bison were hunted. Another Freedman title, *Children of the Wild West* (1983), provides a firsthand look at culture as it was during the settlement of the West.

An exploration of women's roles in each period of U.S. history is found in *American Women—Their Lives in Their Words: A Documentary History* by Doreen Rappaport (1990). Some sections of this collection of fifty first-person accounts are particularly useful with older students.

People and Places

In social studies courses beyond U.S. history, many lively read-aloud possibilities exist.

Noted author Rhoda Blumberg details the 1854 opening of Japan to the United States and examines the deft hand of Commodore Matthew Perry in *Commodore Perry in the Land of the Shogun* (1985). Albert Marrin's story-telling skill continues to be evident in *Aztecs and Spaniards: Cortés and the Conquest of Mexico* (1986).

Alice Fleming's *The King of Prussia and a Peanut Butter Sandwich* (1988) has a far-fetched title but is a well-told story of Mennonite immigration to Kansas from the Crimean Peninsula and the subsequent introduction of the wheat known as Turkey red.

Prairie Visions: The Life and Times of Solomon Butcher by Pam Conrad (1991) paints a moving portrait of turn-of-the-century Nebraska as it presents the life of a pioneer photographer. Conrad uses vivid prose with telling effect to offer a strong sense of time and place.

The graceful prose of *The Wright Brothers: How They Invented the Airplane* by Russell Freedman (1991) captures the winds and sands of Kitty Hawk and the bicycle shop in Dayton, Ohio. Freedman tells in triumphant detail how the Wright brothers solved the mystery of flight.

The distinct moods of the various New England seasons come to life in Gail Gibbons's *Surrounded by Sea: Life on a New England Fishing Island* (1991). The work lends itself as a read-aloud in introducing regions of the United States or as a story-starter for writing activities.

Brent Ashabranner's *Vanishing Border: A Photographic Journey along Our Frontier with Mexico* (1987), rich with anecdotal detail, describes the symbiotic natural history of the area along the two-thousand-mile border between Mexico and the United States.

Native Peoples

Village of the Blue Stone by Stephen Trimble (1990) gently traces life in an Anasazi community some nine hundred years ago. Byrd Baylor's *When Clay Sings*

(1972) can be used to introduce activities related to Native American crafts.

In *People of the Breaking Day* (1990), Marcia Sewall employs a poetic text to recreate the lifeways of the Wampanoags before the *Mayflower* arrived. Two graceful books by Charlotte and David Yue, *The Igloo* (1988) and *The Pueblo* (1988), explore climate and environment as they affect dwelling and culture.

Treasure Trove

Sea Rovers: Pirates, Privateers, and Buccaneers by Albert Marrin (1984) presents lively tales of the men and women who roamed the seas in search of treasure-laden ships. Alvin Schwartz's *Gold and Silver, Silver and Gold: Tales of Hidden Treasure* (1988) reports both true and folkloric accounts of troves of riches and the search for them. Another high-interest title with stories well-told is *Great Mysteries of Ice and Snow* by Edward F. Dolan (1985).

Potpourri

Joan Elma Rahn has a smooth writing style that weaves a cloth rich in detail as she explains the historical roles of horses, rats and fleas, and the American beaver in *Animals that Changed History* (1986).

The lyrical text of Karla Kuskin's *Jerusalem, Shining Still* (1987) makes it a memorable book. *Skara Brae: Story of a Prehistoric Village* by Oliver Dunrea (1985) provides a detailed account of the history of an archeological site in the Orkney Islands.

A final high-interest title that can also expand awareness is *Maggie by My Side* by Beverly Butler (1987). This first-person account recounts the training of a seeing-eye dog as she and her blind owner become a team.

References

Ashabranner, Brent. *Vanishing Border: A Photographic Journey along Our Frontier with Mexico.* New York: G. P. Putnam's Sons, 1987.

Baylor, Byrd. *When Clay Sings.* New York: Charles Scribner's Sons, 1972.

Blumberg, Rhoda. *Commodore Perry in the Land of the Shogun.* New York: Lothrop, Lee and Shepard Books, 1985.

_____. *The Incredible Journey of Lewis and Clark.* New York: Lothrop, Lee and Shepard Books, 1987.

Brown, Drollene P. *Sybil Rides for Independence.* Morton Grove, Ill.: Albert Whitman and Co., 1985.

Brown, Margaret Wise. *Homes in the Wilderness: A Pilgrim's Journal of Plymouth Plantation in 1620 by William Bradford and Others of the Mayflower Company.* Hamden, Conn.: Shoe String Press, Linnet Books, 1988.

Butler, Beverly. *Maggie by My Side.* New York: G. P. Putnam's Sons, 1987.

Conrad, Pam. *Prairie Visions: The Life and Times of Solomon Butcher.* New York: HarperCollins Publishers, 1991.

Dolan, Edward F. *Great Mysteries of Ice and Snow.* New York: G. P. Putnam's Sons, 1985.

Dunrea, Oliver. *Skara Brae: Story of a Prehistoric Village.* New York: Holiday House, 1985.

Faber, Doris, and Harold Faber. *The Birth of a Nation: The Early Years of the United States.* New York: Charles Scribner's Sons, 1989.

Fleming, Alice. *The King of Prussia and a Peanut Butter Sandwich.* New York: Charles Scribner's Sons, 1988.

Freedman, Russell. *Children of the Wild West.* New York: Clarion Books, 1983.

_____. *Buffalo Hunt.* New York: Holiday House, 1988.

Fritz, Jean. *Shh! We're Writing the Constitution.* New York: G. P. Putnam's Sons, 1987.

Gibbons, Gail. *Surrounded by Sea: Life on a New England Fishing Island.* Boston: Little, Brown and Co., 1991.

Kuskin, Karla. *Jerusalem, Shining Still.* New York: Harper and Row, 1987.

Marrin, Albert. *Sea Rovers: Pirates, Privateers, and Buccaneers.* New York: Macmillan Publishing Co., Atheneum Publishers, 1984.

_____. *1812: The War Nobody Won.* New York: Macmillan Publishing Co., Atheneum Publishers, 1985.

_____. *Aztecs and Spaniards: Cortés and the Conquest of Mexico.* New York: Macmillan Publishing Co., Atheneum Publishers, 1986.

_____. *The War for Independence: The Story of the American Revolution.* New York: Macmillan Publishing Co., Atheneum Publishers, 1988.

Meltzer, Milton. *Voices from the Civil War: A Documentary History of the Great American Conflict.* New York: Thomas Y. Crowell, 1989.

Rahn, Joan Elma. *Animals that Changed History.* New York: Macmillan Publishing Co., Atheneum Publishers, 1986.

Rappaport, Doreen. *American Women—Their Lives in Their Words: A Documentary History.* New York: HarperCollins Publishers, 1990.

_____. *Escape from Slavery: Five Journeys to Freedom.* New York: HarperCollins Publishers, 1991.

Roop, Peter, and Connie Roop. *Buttons for General Washington.* Minneapolis, Minn.: Carolrhoda Books, 1986.

Schwartz, Alvin. *Gold and Silver, Silver and Gold: Tales of Hidden Treasure.* New York: HarperCollins Publishers, 1988.

Sewall, Marcia. *The Pilgrims of Plimoth.* New York: Macmillan Publishing Co., Atheneum Publishers, 1986.

_____. *People of the Breaking Day.* New York: Macmillan Publishing Co., Atheneum Publishers, 1990.

Stewart, George. *The Pioneers Go West.* New York: Random House, 1982.

Trimble, Stephen. *Village of the Blue Stone.* New York: Macmillan Publishing Co., 1990.

Trelease, Jim. *The New Read-Aloud Handbook.* New York: Penguin USA, 1989.

Yue, Charlotte, and David Yue. *The Pueblo.* Boston: Houghton Mifflin Co., 1986.

_____. *The Igloo.* Boston: Houghton Mifflin Co., 1988.

Chapter Two

One Hundred Notable Picture Books in the Field of Social Studies

Cherryl Sage

Picture books are an important resource for elementary and middle school social studies teachers. Carefully chosen picture books present compelling stories that invite students to identify with and care about social studies content. Because students can complete several picture books during a class, they can read many stories focusing on a single event or theme to stimulate thoughtful discussion and to invite interesting comparisons and contrasts. In addition, the quality graphics characteristic of notable picture books provide teachers with a refreshing alternative to films and videos.

Selection Criteria

The following bibliography provides a starting point for developing a collection of picture books for the K–8 classroom. Books chosen for this bibliography are currently in print and have appeared on the National Council for the Social Studies-Children's Book Council Notable Children's Trade Books in the Field of Social Studies lists during the years 1978–91.

In general, these books were chosen for the following reasons: they present students with well-written stories told from an interesting perspective, they include graphics that enrich the text, and they present social studies content that is consistently included in the curriculum. Books on this list do not represent thorough coverage of any particular topic nor is there balanced representation of ethnic groups or historical time periods. Rather, these works represent the author's choice of the one hundred best picture books in social studies based on literary and informational quality.

Fiction

Fictional stories cause events and places to come alive in the imagination of students. Using fiction in social studies brings to life content that students have often found irrelevant and uninteresting. In *My Daddy Was a Soldier* (Ray 1990), for example, students experience World War II as a child describes the home-front war efforts including victory gardens, scrap drives, working mothers, and rationing.

Geography becomes more than abstract dots on a map when students hear stories of faraway places such as Cairo in *The Day of Ahmed's Secret* (Heide and Gilliland 1990), or closer-to-home places such as Baltimore in *Chita's Christmas Tree* (Howard 1989). Understanding the multiplicity of relationships and feelings people share becomes concrete in *Old Henry* (Blos 1987). *Ox-Cart Man* (Hall 1979) helps students to create concrete images of the cycle of time and *Mary McLean and the Saint Patrick's Day Parade* (Kroll 1991) helps them appreciate the historical implications of holidays.

Historical Encounters

Bisel, Sarah C. *The Secrets of Vesuvius.* New York: Scholastic, 1991. The author recreates the eruption of Mount Vesuvius in A.D. 79 by presenting the archeological evidence and then using that evidence to invent a compelling story.

Bunting, Eve. *The Wall.* Illustrated by Ronald Himler. New York: Clarion Books, 1990. A boy and his father visit the Vietnam Veterans' Memorial in Washington, D.C.

Cohen, Barbara. *Molly's Pilgrim.* Illustrated by Michael Deraney. New York: William Morrow and Co., 1983. Paperback reprint. New York: Bantam Books, 1990. Molly, a Jewish emigrant from Russia, helps her classmates to expand their definition of pilgrims.

Maruki, Toshi. *Hiroshima No Pika.* New York: Lothrop, Lee and Shepard Books, 1980. In this story, the events of August 6, 1945, become an awful reality.

Ray, Deborah Kogan. *My Daddy Was a Soldier: A World War II Story*. New York: Holiday House, 1990. A child tells about the effects of World War II on the U.S. home front.

Sanders, Scott Russell. *Aurora Means Dawn*. Illustrated by Jill Kastner. New York: Bradbury Press, 1989. The story of a pioneer family that traveled from Connecticut to Ohio in 1800.

Winter, Jeanette. *Follow the Drinking Gourd*. New York: Knopf, 1988. A sailor and conductor on the Underground Railroad teaches slaves a folk song that becomes their guide to freedom.

A Sense of Place

Andrews, Jan. *Very Last First Time*. Illustrated by Ian Wallace. New York: Macmillan Publishing Co., 1985. A story that holds the magic of two places— an Inuit village in Northern Canada and the sea bottom covered only by a thick roof of ice.

Heide, Florence Parry, and Judith Heide Gilliland. *The Day of Ahmed's Secret*. Illustrated by Ted Lewin. New York: Lothrop, Lee and Shepard Books, 1990. Readers are held spellbound by the sights, sounds, and smells of Cairo as they wait to hear Ahmed's secret.

Howard, Elizabeth Fitzgerald. *Chita's Christmas Tree*. Illustrated by Floyd Cooper. New York: Bradbury Press, 1989. The story of Chita's Christmas tree is told in turn-of-the-century Baltimore.

McKissack, Patricia. *Mirandy and Brother Wind*. Illustrated by Jerry Pinkney. New York: Alfred A. Knopf, 1988. Move back in time to the South in the early 1900s and join Mirandy in a cakewalk— a dance competition rooted in African-American culture.

Smucker, Anna. *No Star Nights*. Paintings by Steve Johnson. New York: Alfred A. Knopf, 1989. A young girl growing up in the 1950s describes the rhythm of life in a small steel-mill town.

Weir, Bob, and Wendy Weir. *Panther Dream*. New York: Hyperion, 1991. The illustrations and audio tape that accompany this book bring the African rain forest to life for students.

Special Relationships

Blos, Joan W. *Old Henry*. Illustrated by Stephen Gammell. New York: William Morrow and Co., 1987. To Henry, his house is just the right amount of messy, but to Henry's neighbors the house is a disgrace. With just the right amount of compromise, Henry and his neighbors learn to celebrate their differences.

Caines, Jeannette. *Just Us Women*. Illustrated by Pat Cummings. New York: HarperCollins Publishers, 1982. A warm relationship between a young girl and her aunt unfolds as they enjoy a trip for women only.

Durrell, Ann, and Marilyn Sachs, eds. *The Big Book for Peace*. New York: Penguin USA, Dutton Children's Books, 1990. This collection of stories, poems, and artwork by noted children's authors and illustrators explores the many dimensions of peace.

MacLachlan, Patricia. *Mama One, Mama Two*. Illustrated by Ruth Bornstein. New York: HarperCollins Publishers, 1982. A foster mother tells a story of love and reassurance to her "for a while child." Also recommended is another book by the same author: *Through Grandpa's Eyes*. Illustrated by Deborah Ray. New York: HarperCollins Publishers, 1980.

Madenski, Melissa. *Some of the Pieces*. Illustrated by Deborah Ray. Boston: Little, Brown and Co., 1991. During the year after their father's death, two young children and their mother share memories and begin to rebuild their lives.

The Cycle of Time

Baker, Jeannie. *Window*. New York: William Morrow and Co., Greenwillow Books, 1991. A wordless picture book that captures the cycle of change from wilderness to city through a series of vibrant collages.

Hall, Donald. *Ox-Cart Man*. Illustrated by Barbara Cooney. New York: Penguin USA, Viking, 1979. A story that depicts the cycle of the seasons as experienced by a nineteenth-century New England farm family.

Pryor, Bonnie. *The House on Maple Street*. Illustrated by Beth Peck. New York: William Morrow and Co.,

1987. A journey from the present back through three hundred years of history connects the residents of 107 Maple Street to a time when only forest animals lived on the land.

von Tscharner, Renata. *New Providence.* Illustrated by Denis Orloff. San Diego: Harcourt Brace Jovanovich, 1987. Through the use of both text and paintings, this book chronicles the changing face of an imaginary city from 1910 to 1987.

Holiday Stories

Anderson, Joan. *Christmas on the Prairie.* Photographed by George Anderson. New York: Clarion Books, 1985. Christmas on the prairie in 1836 is recreated here accompanied by a lively story based on historical records and photographs taken from the Conner Prairie Pioneer Settlement living history museum. A similar book from the same author and photographer team, *The First Thanksgiving Feast* (Clarion Books, 1984), is also recommended.

dePaola, Tomie. *Tony's Bread.* New York: G. P. Putnam's Sons, 1989. A delicious tale of how panettone, the sweet Italian Christmas bread, came to be.

Kimmel, Eric. *Hershel and the Hanukkah Goblins.* Illustrated by Trina Schart Hyman. New York: Holiday House, 1989. Hershel outwits the goblins and restores Hanukkah to the town of Ostropol.

Kroll, Steven. *Mary McLean and the Saint Patrick's Day Parade.* Illustrated by Michael Dooling. New York: Scholastic, 1991. A Saint Patrick's Day tale set in 1850 on Manhattan Island. Historical notes included.

Poetry

Poetry in the social studies classroom uses the rhythm of language to create memorable images of events, ideas, people, and places. Longfellow's famous poem *Paul Revere's Ride* becomes a vivid Revolutionary War image in a picture book illustrated by Ted Rand (1990).

As the poet Robert Southey takes us on a rollicking word trip down the *Cataract of Lodore* (illustrated by Mordicai Gerstein, 1991), listeners develop mental images of geographic features that can be matched only by experience. Poetry also develops vivid images

of people—images that convey the feeling and essence of their lives rather than the mere facts. The people in Eloise Greenfield's African-American neighborhood in *Night on Neighborhood Street* are portrayed as special and strong rather than as stereotypes.

Poetry shared with a class can cause students to laugh, to cry, and to care about social studies content.

Stories and Legends

Baylor, Byrd. *Moon Song.* Illustrated by Ronald Himler. New York: Charles Scribner's Sons, 1982. A Pima Indian legend that sings of the special relationship between Mother Moon and her Coyote children.

Burkert, Nancy. *Valentine and Orson.* New York: Farrar, Straus and Giroux, 1989. A folk play in verse that retells the story of twin brothers separated at birth who join together to fight fearsome monsters and then discover their true identity.

Hartford, John. *Steamboat in a Cornfield.* New York: Crown Publishing Group, 1986. In 1910, before the Ohio River was controlled by locks and dams, a steamboat did indeed land in a cornfield. This ballad turns a news story of that day into a memorable historic event.

Longfellow, Henry Wadsworth. *Paul Revere's Ride.* Illustrated by Ted Rand. New York: Penguin USA, Dutton Children's Books, 1990. Paul Revere's famous ride is brought to life for yet another generation of readers.

Service, Robert. *The Cremation of Sam McGee.* Paintings by Ted Harrison. New York: William Morrow and Co., Greenwillow Books, 1986. A classic poem from Yukon Gold Rush days illustrated with bold, surreal paintings.

Ideas of Note

Paxton, Tom. *Belling the Cat and Other Aesop's Fables.* Illustrated by Robert Rayevsky. New York: William Morrow and Co., 1990. Timeless truths retold in verse, illustrated with bold, full-page graphics.

Jeffers, Susan, illustrator. *Brother Eagle, Sister Sky: A Message from Chief Seattle.* New York: Penguin USA, Dial Books for Young Readers, 1991. A compelling message to care for the earth is illustrated with beautiful, full-color paintings.

Thoreau, Henry David. *Walden.* Text selected by Steve Lowe. Illustrations by Robert Sabuda. New York: Philomel Books, 1990. Linoleum-cut prints enhance the wisdom of Thoreau's reflections on nature, solitude, and life.

Special Places

Agard, John. *The Calypso Alphabet.* Illustrated by Jennifer Bent. New York: Henry Holt and Co., 1989. Poetry in the calypso tradition introduces twenty-six Caribbean sights and sounds.

Siebert, Diane. *Heartland.* Paintings by Wendell Minor. New York: Crowell, 1989. The poem and paintings that illustrate the text create a strong sense of the U.S. Midwest. Also recommended are two similar books by the same author and illustrator team: *Mojave* (Crowell, 1988) and *Sierra* (HarperCollins Publishers, 1991).

Southey, Robert. *The Cataract of Lodore.* Illustrated by Mordicai Gerstein. New York: Penguin USA, Dial Books for Young Readers, 1991. Using vivid word pictures, the poet takes his listeners on a river journey that begins in the "tarn on the fell" and ends at Lodore with a "mighty uproar."

Celebrating People

Greenfield, Eloise. *Night on Neighborhood Street.* Illustrated by Jan Spivey Gilchrist. New York: Penguin USA, Dial Books for Young Readers, 1991. A collection of poems that invite the reader to share the sights and sounds of an evening in an African-American neighborhood.

Griego, Margot. *Tortillitas Para Mama.* Illustrated by Barbara Cooney. New York: Henry Holt and Co., 1981. A collection of Spanish nursery rhymes in both English and Spanish.

Lindbergh, Reeve. *Johnny Appleseed.* Illustrated by Kathy Jakobsen. Boston: Little, Brown and Co., 1990. A biographical poem that tells the story of John Chapman, a naturalist and missionary, who lived from 1774 to 1845.

Morris, Ann. *Bread, Bread, Bread.* Photographs by Ken Heyman. New York: Lothrop, Lee and Shepard Books, 1989. People around the world enjoy bread in its many interesting variations.

Provensen, Alice. *The Buck Stops Here.* New York: HarperCollins Publishers, 1990. Through rhyme and detailed illustrations, students learn about U.S. presidents from George Washington to George Bush.

Nonfiction

Nonfiction books are the most frequent type of literature used in the social studies classroom. The nonfiction books chosen for this bibliography have the special quality of presenting information so that it captures the imagination. *On Top of the World* (Fraser 1991) invites its readers to scale Mount Everest with Sir Edmund Hillary; *The Great Wall of China* (Fisher 1986) becomes an invitation to march with Grand General Meng Tian to build a mighty fortress. In *Teammates* (Golenbock 1990), students feel the barbs of racism while they learn about the history of baseball.

Nonfiction books that cause students to feel a part of historical and geographical adventures are far more appealing to them than strictly factual accounts.

Exploration and Discovery

Fisher, Leonard Everett. *The Great Wall of China.* New York: Macmillan Publishing Co., 1986. The story of the Great Wall of China is told through black-and-white paintings and carefully researched text. Similar books by the same author, *The Tower of London* (Macmillan Publishing Co., 1987) and *The Wailing Wall* (Macmillan Publishing Co., 1989), are also recommended.

Fraser, Mary Ann. *On Top of the World: The Conquest of Mount Everest.* New York: Henry Holt and Co., 1991. An exciting retelling of the 1953 conquest of Mount Everest by Sir Edmund Hillary.

Maestro, Betsy, and Giulio Maestro. *The Discovery of the Americas.* New York: Lothrop, Lee and Shepard Books, 1991. The discovery of the Americas unfolds as the reader learns about Stone Age migrations from Asia to North America, the Phoenician and Viking explorations, and the voyages of Columbus and Cabot.

People: Celebrating Diversity of Experiences

Abells, Chana. *The Children We Remember: Photographs from the Archives of Yad Vashem.* New York: William Morrow and Co., Greenwillow Books, 1986. Elegantly simple text and powerful photographs introduce children to the Holocaust.

Anderson, Joan. *Pioneer Children of Appalachia.* Photographs by George Ancona. Boston: Houghton Mifflin Co., 1986. A recreation of a pioneer family's life, photographed at the living history museum in Fort New Salem, West Virginia.

Ekoomiak, Normee. *Arctic Memories.* New York: Henry Holt and Co., 1990. In both Inuit and English, the author describes his childhood in an Arctic Eskimo village.

Fisher, Leonard Everett. *Prince Henry the Navigator.* New York: Macmillan Publishing Co., 1990. Fisher describes the accomplishments of Prince Henry's school of navigation, which developed the knowledge underlying the ocean-based discoveries of the fifteenth century.

Golenbock, Peter. *Teammates.* Illustrated by Paul Bacon. San Diego: Harcourt Brace Jovanovich, 1990. Jackie Robinson, the first African-American major league baseball player, and his European-American teammate, Pee Wee Reese, stand together against angry fans.

Hoyt-Goldsmith, Diane. *Pueblo Storyteller.* Photographs by Lawrence Migdale. New York: Holiday House, 1991. The traditions of the Pueblo Indians are woven into a story told by April, a child of the Cochiti Pueblo.

Humble, Richard. *The Travels of Marco Polo.* Illustrated by Richard Hook. New York: Franklin Watts, 1990. Clear text presented in an attractive format tells the story of Marco Polo's journeys through Asia and of his famous book, *Travels.*

Jakes, John. *Susanna of the Alamo.* Illustrated by Paul Bacon. San Diego: Harcourt Brace Jovanovich, 1986. Susanna Dickenson survived the Battle of the Alamo and then undertook a perilous journey to tell the story of that bloody battle to General Sam Houston.

Keegan, Marcia. *Pueblo Boy: Growing Up in Two Worlds.* New York: Penguin USA, Dutton Children's Books, 1991. Through photographs and text, Timmy Roybal shares his life as a typical 10-year-old and as a Pueblo Indian in San Ildefonso, New Mexico.

Say, Allen. *El Chino.* Boston: Houghton Mifflin Co., 1990. The biography of Bong Way Wong, the first Chinese bullfighter.

Stanley, Fay. *The Last Princess: The Story of Princess Ka'iulani of Hawai'i.* Illustrated by Diane Stanley. New York: Four Winds Press, 1991. An account of a princess who fought bravely to preserve her people's freedom and of U.S. annexation of the Hawaiian Islands.

Waters, Kate. *Sarah Morton's Day: A Day in the Life of a Pilgrim Girl.* Photographed by Russ Kendall. New York: Scholastic, 1989. Photographs from the living history museum at Plimoth Plantation highlight the story of Sarah Morton, a pilgrim child in 1627.

Folklore

When used in the teaching of social studies, fables, legends, and folktales become more than simply an interesting literary genre. Fables—didactic stories that frequently have stated morals—offer students access to a storehouse of cultural values. Myths and legends, which use the symbols of a culture to explain the mysterious and otherwise unexplainable, provide the student with a sense of a culture's metaphysics.

Folktales allow students to experience one of the ways a society develops a sense of moral behavior in its children. The folk literature section is arranged here by geographic region so that teachers can easily integrate the stories into the study of history and geography.

The Americas

Ada, Alma. *The Gold Coin.* Illustrated by Neil Waldman. New York: Macmillan Publishing Co., Atheneum Publishers, 1991. Dona Josefa teaches Juan, a thief for more than thirty years, about a human treasure more valuable than gold.

Alexander, Ellen. *Llama and the Great Flood: A Folktale from Peru.* New York: Crowell, 1989.

The tale of how a llama saved his owner from a great flood that destroyed the world.

Flora. *Feathers like a Rainbow: An Amazon Indian Tale*. New York: HarperCollins Publishers, 1989. The drab, dark birds of a long ago, faraway jungle search for a way to have feathers as colorful as the flowers that surround them.

Goble, Paul. *Beyond the Ridge*. New York: Bradbury Press, 1989. The Plains Indian vision of death and an afterlife are conveyed through sensitive text and rich paintings. Also recommended are two other Indian legends by the same author: *Buffalo Woman* (Bradbury Press, 1984) and *The Girl Who Loved Wild Horses* (Macmillan Publishing Co., 1978).

Hooks, William. *The Ballad of Belle Dorcas*. Illustrated by Brian Pinkney. New York: Alfred A. Knopf, 1990. Belle, a conjure woman, uses her magic to keep her love with her always.

Lattimore, Deborah. *The Flame of Peace*. New York: HarperCollins Publishers, 1987. An Aztec boy overcomes the nine evil lords of darkness to obtain the flame of peace for his people.

Lionni, Leo. *Tillie and the Wall*. New York: Alfred A. Knopf, 1989. Tillie bravely ventures to the other side of the wall to discover, much to her surprise, that ordinary mice live there. Other recommended animal fables by the same author include *Six Crows* (Alfred A. Knopf, 1988) and *Nicholas, Where Have You Been?* (Alfred A. Knopf, 1987).

Roth, Susan. *The Story of Light*. New York: William Morrow and Co., 1990. This story, inspired by a Cherokee myth, is appropriately illustrated with vibrant yellow and black woodcuts.

San Souci, Robert. *The Legend of Scarface: A Blackfeet Indian Tale*. Illustrated by Daniel San Souci. New York: Doubleday, 1978. A disfigured Indian youth who is kind to all he meets earns the right to ask a favor of the sun. *Song of Sedna* (Doubleday, 1981), an Eskimo legend by the same author and illustrator team, is also recommended.

Seeger, Pete. *Abiyoyo*. Illustrations by Michael Hays. New York: Macmillan Publishing Co., 1986. Banished from town because of their music and magic, a little boy and his father use those very same tools to rid the town of the fearsome giant Abiyoyo.

Shetterly, Susan. *Raven's Light: A Myth from the People of the Northwest Coast*. Illustrated by Robert Shetterly. New York: Macmillan Publishing Co., 1991. In this creation myth, Raven makes the earth, animals, moon, and sun.

Europe

Climo, Shirley. *King of the Birds*. Illustrated by Ruth Heller. New York: Crowell, 1988. Found in various forms throughout the world, this ancient story tells how wren became king of the birds and ordered the earth so that the birds could live in peace.

Croll, Carolyn. *The Three Brothers: A German Folktale*. New York: G. P. Putnam's Sons, 1989. Three brothers compete to fill a barn in order to inherit their father's farm.

Fisher, Leonard Everett. *Theseus and the Minotaur*. New York: Holiday House, 1988. This Greek myth about the battle between Theseus and the bull-headed monster, the Minotaur, is retold and beautifully illustrated with full-color paintings.

Jacobs, Joseph. *Tattercoats*. Illustrated by Margo Tomes. New York: G. P. Putnam's Sons, 1989. This is a version of a traditional English tale, similar to the French "Cinderella." Also recommended: Shirley Climo's *The Egyptian Cinderella*, illustrated by Ruth Heller (Crowell, 1989).

Lattimore, Deborah. *The Sailor Who Captured the Sea*. New York: HarperCollins Publishers, 1991. In this original story, students come to know the Book of Kells, hear of an artist's struggle to find his own voice, and wonder at the extraordinary art that embellishes every page.

Rogasky, Barbara. *The Water of Life*. Illustrated by Trina Schart Hyman. New York: Holiday House, 1986. In a tale of treachery, pride, and happily ever after, a young prince searches for the water of life to cure his ill father.

Talbott, Hudson. *King Arthur: The Sword and the Stone*. New York: William Morrow and Co., 1991. A retelling of the Arthurian legend for young listeners that captures the spirit of the tale with imaginative language and bold illustrations.

Wisniewski, David. *Elfwyn's Saga*. New York: Lothrop,

Lee and Shepard Books, 1990. A story, based on an Icelandic legend, of a blind child who is blessed with the gift of vision.

Africa

Aardema, Verna. *Bringing the Rain to Kapiti Plain.* Illustrated by Beatriz Vidal. New York: Penguin USA, Dial Books for Young Readers, 1981. An African cumulative tale with a rhythm similar to "This Is the House that Jack Built." Also recommended by the same author: *Traveling to Tondo: A Tale of the Nkundo of Zaire*, illustrated by Will Hillenbrand (Alfred A. Knopf, 1991).

Grifalconi, Ann. *The Village of Round and Square Houses.* Boston: Little, Brown and Co., 1986. The story of a real village in Central Africa where the men live in square houses and the women live in round houses.

Mollel, Tololwa. *The Orphan Boy.* Illustrated by Paul Morin. New York: Clarion Books, 1990. A Maasai story that explains why Venus is known in Africa as Kileken or the Orphan Boy.

Steptoe, John. *Mufaro's Beautiful Daughters: An African Tale.* New York: Lothrop, Lee and Shepard Books, 1987. Mufaro has two beautiful daughters, one kind and one vain. Which will the king choose for a wife?

Asia

Birdeye, Tom. *A Song of Stars: An Asian Legend.* Illustrated by Ju-Hong Chen. New York: Holiday House, 1990. The legend of the annual reunion of two lovers who were banished to opposite ends of the Milky Way because their love caused them to neglect their work. In China, the day of their meeting is called the Festival of the Milky Way; in Japan, it is called the Weaving Loom Festival or Tanabata.

Lee, Jeanne. *Toad Is the Uncle of Heaven: A Vietnamese Folktale.* New York: Henry Holt and Co., 1985. Toad brings rain to Earth and is granted the title Uncle of Heaven.

Marshak, Samuel. *The Month-Brothers.* Illustrated by Diane Stanley. New York: William Morrow and Co., 1983. The retelling of a Slavic story in which a girl, ordered by her cruel stepmother to find delicate spring flowers in the middle of the winter, meets the Month-Brothers.

Peaver, Richard. *Our King Has Horns!* Illustrated by Robert Rayevsky. New York: Macmillan Publishing Co., 1987. This Georgian folktale illustrates that the truth will not go away no matter what the punishment for hiding it.

Rodanas, Kristina. *The Story of Wali Dad.* New York: William Morrow and Co., 1988. The surprising results of a single generous action are recounted in this story based on an Indian tale.

Wang, Rosalin. *The Fourth Question: A Chinese Tale.* Illustrated by Ju-Hong Chen. New York: Holiday House, 1991. A journey to visit the Wise Man yields answers to three of Yee-Lee's questions. His fourth question is answered because of his kindness and good deeds.

Young, Ed. *Lon Po Po: A Red-Riding Hood Story from China.* New York: Philomel Books, 1989. An Asian version of the classic fairy tale illustrated with Chinese panel art.

Conclusion

Using various types of literature in the social studies curriculum encourages students to experience, feel, and know the content in a variety of forms. With this goal of fostering more complex understandings in mind, the purpose of this bibliography is to provide teachers and media specialists a selection guide to some of the best available picture books in the field of social studies.

Chapter Three

Great Geography Using Notable Trade Books

Robert Stremme

The five fundamental themes in geography are contained in *Guidelines for Geographic Education: Elementary and Secondary Schools* (Committee on Geographic Education 1984), a booklet prepared by the Association of American Geographers and the National Council for Geographic Education. These five themes include location, place, human-environment interactions (relationships within places), movement (relationships between places), and regions. Using these five fundamental themes, a teacher can create interrelated geography lessons and make geography meaningful for students.

The National Council for the Social Studies-Children's Book Council Joint Committee reviews and nominates outstanding children's trade books in which the five themes of geography appear repeatedly and that are thus useful in teaching geography. Without *stressing* the themes, these trade books nonetheless manage to weave geography into the narrative. Each year, the NCSS-CBC Notable list contains nonfiction books specific to geographic places, providing excellent opportunities to incorporate children's trade books into the curriculum.

The books selected for this chapter are, for the most part, picture books and storybooks. Teachers can use these books for independent reading, oral classroom presentation, or small-group sharing. Each book contains many of the five geographic themes within its structure. Together, they serve as a few examples of how trade books can be used to augment the instruction of classroom geography.

Location and Place

From maps we can learn the geographic theme of location. For example, we can learn the absolute location of a place like New York City. The ability to find a particular absolute location helps students find their way from place to place around the globe. Unfortunately, knowing where a specific landform is located does not automatically lead to understanding it. Using trade books at this point helps the students to remember the characteristics of the various themes of geography.

On Top of the World: The Conquest of Mount Everest by Mary Ann Fraser (1991) begins by offering students an excellent example of a location. Mount Everest can be identified by specific latitude and longitude coordinates. Most students can successfully locate it on their maps and then learn about its legendary height. This simply written text takes intermediate grade students on the last push that Sir Edmund Hillary and Tenzing Norgay made as they conquered Mount Everest. Few readers will experience a mountain climb of this magnitude, but they can experience the mountain climbers' feelings of despair and elation by learning about the formidable characteristics of this place and about how humans and the environment interact in harsh circumstances.

Another geographic location, which includes a tragic history of human-environment interaction, can be found in Herculaneum, Italy. In A.D. 79, Mount Vesuvius buried this ancient city under layers of lava. Sara C. Bisel presents her account of this event in *The Secrets of Vesuvius* (1991). Students can pinpoint the location of this landform and date the eruption. The intermediate grade reader gets a complete package in this book. Part of the narrative contains a fictional account of a slave girl as she completes her chores on that last day. The students gain a sense of history as they read how environmental characteristics shaped the everyday chores of the townspeople. This historical fiction, interspersed with factual chapters, shows pictures of the archeologist's work and the physical geography of the volcano. The reader will learn how the skeletal remains of a female cradling a baby can be identified as those of a slave. Volcanoes seem to hold endless fascination for elementary students and this notable book answers many questions that students ask about volcanoes.

Seeing Earth from Space by Patricia Lauber (1990) provides excellent overhead views of absolute and relative locations. Atolls, sand dunes, reefs, and salt flats look different when seen from a bird's-eye view. Using remote sensing devices, the author includes unusual pictures of the absolute locations of, for example, the source and mouth of the Mississippi River and the extent of the Grand Canyon. Different from the traditional textbook approach, this overhead view can redefine familiar geographic terms.

Place

The physical and human characteristics of a geographical area define a place. Place geography helps children identify with specific surroundings as well as relate the names given to places that might reflect their characteristics. Children learn quickly to identify *their* place in, for example, the classroom or the school.

Sahara: Vanishing Cultures by Jan Reynolds (1991) does an excellent job of showing the characteristics of desert places. Color photographs make the desert a place of beauty while simple text explains how the Turaeg people exist in this barren land. Pictures of hairy goatskin water bags and hobbled camels teach students about cultures they may find difficult to understand. The physical surroundings of the Sahara combined with the nomadic peoples show the distinctiveness of this place. After reading this book, students can look at their own place and write down its distinguishing human and physical geographic features.

For many children, the earth itself holds a special fascination. Primary school children will appreciate the message of *On the Day You Were Born* by Debra Frasier (1991). This picture book tells of the marvelous things waiting to happen to the unborn baby. Geographical concepts such as tides, gravity, and air are presented and explained in simple terms. Each picture shows the newborn child interacting with the geographic environment. The illustrations of children show a multicultural population. This book could be used in the study of the earth's rotation and as a springboard for students to identify other happenings that occurred in their world on the day they were born.

Primary school children will especially enjoy the humor in *My Place in Space* by Robin and Sally Hirst

(1990). In this book, Henry asks the bus driver to take him home. The bus driver asks Henry if he can locate his home. To the astonished driver, Henry reels off his Australian address by planet, solar system, galaxy, cluster, and universe. Young students quickly understand how geography can be used to locate place in the sky. This book helps students place themselves in the complex geographic universe.

Human-Environment Interactions

Human-environment interactions show how people form relationships with the physical and cultural surroundings *within* a place. When people drain a swamp to prepare the ground for construction, a change in the geography takes place. As humans interact with the environment, subtle and drastic geographic changes occur. Some of these interactions form a positive relationship whereas others lead to negative changes in the world. This theme offers endless possibilities for integrated teaching in the elementary subject areas.

Window by Jeannie Baker (1991) offers a wordless look into the changing face of geography. Here, a mother and infant look out of the bedroom window at the countryside. The dirt road in front of the house, bordered by woods, seems to go nowhere in particular. Over a space of twenty years, the boy watches the geography change outside his bedroom window. A forest becomes a field that gives way to suburbs. The suburban landscape evolves into a city that bears no resemblance to the woods of twenty years ago. On the last page, the boy, now a young man, looks at the countryside from a window in his new home and the cycle continues. This simple, wordless picture book offers students opportunities to see the dynamic nature of geography. The view-from-the-window approach lends itself to many lesson applications. For example, primary school students can view a lake or pond during various seasons of the year and can observe how it and its surroundings change. Teachers can challenge students to take the point of view of a rain forest animal and document in pictures and words the changes that occur in this geographical setting. Classes that communicate through letters or telecommunication can share the geography outside their school windows. The ocean view outside the school in coastal New Jersey would fascinate students in a Midwestern school. They, in turn, could offer the sea of a grassy plain for comparison.

The Land of Gray Wolf by Thomas Locker (1991) uses beautiful paintings and prose to demonstrate how the native tribes of North America respected and preserved their environment. Running Deer and his father, Gray Wolf, carefully use their environment and watch as the new settlers carelessly destroy it. The land undergoes tragic transformations as the settlers use it up and move on to new territory. Although the story could end there, Running Deer sees hope as the land revitalizes itself. Because students often see geography in absolute terms, this narrative will help them understand the changing nature of land use. Teachers can challenge children to find local examples of geography that are changing and identify causes and effects.

Primary grade children will enjoy the interaction of *The Old Ladies Who Liked Cats* by Carol Greene (1991). In whimsical fable fashion, an island com-

The Old Ladies Who Liked Cats
By Carol Greene Pictures By Loretta Krupinski

From *The Old Ladies Who Liked Cats*, © 1991 illustrations by Loretta Krupinski, reprinted by permission of HarperCollins Publishers.

munity overcomes human invaders by once again allowing the cats to roam outside at night. The old ladies of the land understand how the geography of their island can be changed by altering the way humans and their environment interact. The wise women put things right again and become the real heroes. This book provides a wonderful starting

point for many lessons in geography. Students can search for historical examples of cultures that have faded away because of altered geography and propose new endings that would preserve the geography.

Movement

Movement (relationships between places) examines how natural processes, people, goods, and ideas travel from place to place. Illustrating movement can be as simple as showing how a locally produced product is shipped to the next town.

The Stream by Naomi Russell (1991) offers a look into the movement of the water cycle. Rain falls on the mountains and seeps underground. Then it travels through the land, forming streams, rivers, and lakes. Along the way, this movement of water changes the land and people it touches. Finally, the water flows into the ocean and evaporates into the sky to become rain again. The illustrations in this small, simple picture book hold a wealth of detail. Without mentioning the terms, this book teaches *source, mouth, tributary, condensation,* and *evaporation.* Young children could illustrate the terms as they come to understand the definitions. Teachers can build a complete water cycle lesson using this book as a starting point.

Ulco Glimmerveen's *A Tale of Antarctica* (1990) offers a powerful message about movement. At first glance this colorful picture book looks like a whimsical tale of a penguin thinking about humans arriving in Antarctica. As the students study the book and focus on movement, however, several questions come into focus. How did the trash get to the shores of Antarctica? When the humans leave, why does the pollution get worse? Perhaps this simple children's book will connect students with the movement of trash they thoughtlessly heave into the waterways.

Two picture books about cities offer the opportunity to compare and contrast the movement of goods, services, and ideas. *Wake Up City!* by Alvin Tresselt (1990) and *The Day of Ahmed's Secret* by Florence Parry Heide and Judith Heide Gilliland (1990) both follow the movement of a city as it comes to life. The city movement includes people, animals, goods, money, and ideas. Tresselt's city could be "Anywhere, U.S.A."; Ahmed specifically explores Cairo, Egypt.

Besides having students point out the geographic themes found in these cities, the differences between them can be noted and expanded.

Regions

Regions consist of areas that have physical or humanly created attributes that make them distinctive from their surroundings. The Great Plains, with its extensive grasslands, for example, can be easily identified as a region differing from the mountainous Rocky Mountains to the west. These two areas are geographically unique because of their physical characteristics.

Sugaring Time by Kathryn Lasky (1990) tells the story of a region unique in all the world. The sugar maple trees of northeastern North America form a region that also has definite seasonal patterns. This text, accompanied by black-and-white photographs, explains the process of making maple syrup. Children can identify the geographic area of the maple sugar trees and discover why the characteristics of this region, because of its vegetation and climatic patterns, are distinctive. The fascinating process of tapping sugar maples toward the end of winter produces a regional food product dear to the hearts of most children.

The climate and vegetation of the rain forests form another geographic region that children find intriguing. Most students already have a picture of a tropical rain forest in their minds just from hearing the words *rain forest*. Have the students draw their versions of a rain forest, display them without comment, and then read *Regina's Big Mistake* by Marissa Moss (1990). In this book, Regina starts drawing her rain forest, but when it doesn't match the pictures of the other students she feels compelled to change it repeatedly. Because she must continue to make these changes on the same sheet of paper, her rain forest becomes unique. Regina learns that creativity and geography can be compatible. For older students, follow this lesson with a reading of *One Day in the Tropical Rain Forest* by Jean Craighead George (1990). This minute-by-minute account tells how a native guide and a scientist save a portion of the rain forest when they finally sight an unnamed butterfly. The students will appreciate this adventurous narrative while learning about varied aspects of the rain forest region. This region, in particular, is one environmental puzzle demanding that all the pieces fit to be complete. Have the students take one part of the narrative and finish the ending another way to see how the region could change.

Creative Geography Teaching

Creative geography teaching incorporates children's trade books. These few notable titles serve as examples of the wealth of material available for all grade levels. By identifying the characteristics of the five fundamental themes of geography from notable children's trade books, teachers enable students to experience the richness of a fascinating subject.

References

Baker, Jeannie. *Window*. New York: William Morrow and Co., Greenwillow Books, 1991.

Bisel, Sara C. *The Secrets of Vesuvius*. New York: Scholastic, 1991.

Committee on Geographic Education, National Council for Geographic Education and Association of American Geographers. *Guidelines for Geographic Education: Elementary and Secondary Schools*. Washington, D.C., and Macomb, Ill.: Association of American Geographers and National Council for Geographic Education, 1984.

Fraser, Mary Ann. *On Top of the World: The Conquest of Mount Everest*. New York: Henry Holt and Co., 1991.

Frasier, Debra. *On the Day You Were Born*. San Diego: Harcourt Brace Jovanovich, 1991.

George, Jean Craighead. *One Day in the Tropical Rain Forest*. New York: HarperCollins Publishers, 1990.

Glimmerveen, Ulco. *A Tale of Antarctica*. New York: Scholastic, 1990.

Greene, Carol. *The Old Ladies Who Liked Cats*. New York: HarperCollins Publishers, 1991.

Heide, Florence Parry, and Judith Heide Gilliland. *The Day of Ahmed's Secret*. New York: Scholastic, 1990.

Hirst, Robin, and Sally Hirst. *My Place in Space*. New York: Orchard Books, 1990.

Lasky, Kathryn. *Sugaring Time*. New York: Aladdin Books, 1990.

Lauber, Patricia. *Seeing Earth from Space*. New York: Orchard Books, 1990.

Locker, Thomas. *The Land of Gray Wolf*. New York: Penguin USA, Dial Books for Young Readers, 1991.

Moss, Marissa. *Regina's Big Mistake*. Boston: Houghton Mifflin Co., 1990.

National Geographic Society, The. "Maps, the Landscape, and Fundamental Themes in Geography." Map/Brochure. Washington, D.C.: National Geographic Society, 1986.

Reynolds, Jan. *Sahara: Vanishing Cultures*. San Diego: Harcourt Brace Jovanovich, 1991.

Russell, Naomi. *The Stream*. New York: Penguin USA, Dutton Children's Books, 1991.

Tresselt, Alvin. *Wake Up, City!* New York: Lothrop, Lee and Shepard Books, 1990.

Chapter Four

New Biographies Are "Better than Before"

Shirley Wilton

Biographies for children are not generally regarded as great or important works of literature. Children are supposed to like them because they are stories of real people, and teachers are apt to think of them as easy sources of information. For some teachers, biographies are easy assignments. "Write a report on Benjamin Franklin," or "Find three famous women," or "Who was Tecumseh?" Juvenile biography wears the dull mantle of predictability. At best it is thought to be useful. At worst it is thought to oversimplify and fictionalize the lives of important people.

Early Biographies

Unfortunately, there is reason for biography's mundane reputation in the world of children's books. Particularly in the early years of the genre, scholarship and authenticity faded before the perceived need to find role models in history. Famous people were turned into model citizens and examples of right behavior who "seemed[ed] merely to have passed through the Ten Commandments, nodding dutifully to each one of them" (Wibberley 1962, 20). Past lives were sadly skewed by the omission of any mention of human failings and often, in an attempt to interest young readers, authors added fictive dialogue and drama.

Many of these early biographies were packaged in the uniform format and writing style mandated by a publisher's series—simply written, fictionalized, and formulaic. The Bobbs-Merrill Childhood of Famous Americans series was popular with children and their teachers for its charming tales of how great men and women learned young the moral truths and social roles that would bring them fame in later life. Betsy Ross, for example, learned that sewing was more appropriate for her than her brother's carpentry and that, as a girl, she should not wish for "things that can never be," but should be happy "just being herself" (Weil 1954, 22–23).

Some of these early biographies are still on the library shelves, and some of the prize-winning titles are still routinely recommended to children of the 1990s. The writing still holds interest, but the lessons upheld by the books written during the 1950s, for example, ring with a false note today. *Amos Fortune, Free Man* (Yates 1950) won the Newbery award in 1951. Today it reads like a satire of the "good slave." Amos Fortune, an African prince, captured at age 15 and sold into slavery, moved to New England with his owner, bought his freedom, and became a hard-working, self-denying, ever-humble citizen—a Calvinist with black skin who, in his will, bequeathed a silver communion service to the local church. James Daugherty's *Daniel Boone* (1939), another Newbery winner, is full of action and adventure and lively writing. But Daugherty's Indians are "red varmints," sullen savages who attack the white settlers with tomahawks and scalp knives.

These early biographies fall into a type described in 1973 by Patrick Groff as "romantic" or "heroic" biographies, intended to offer role models of patriotism, diligence, and proper behavior. But revolutions in our social consciousness have occurred since they were written, and more recent titles reflect the vast changes that have occurred in U.S. society.

Current Biographies

Biographies written for children today are more realistic in their portrayal of famous men and women. The books are likely to be products of extensive research and many meet the high standards now expected in nonfiction writing. Juvenile biographies have radically changed as a result of increased critical attention, as well as changing educational philosophies. The genre has attracted talented writers, illustrators, and book designers. The best examples of the new biography can equal fiction, folk literature, and other forms of writing in encouraging learning, critical thinking, and open discussion. With the emphasis on whole language and the literature-based curriculum, the genre today offers an exciting source of materials for classroom teachers.

The revolution in biographical writing for children began in the early 1970s, just at the time the National Council for the Social Studies-Children's Book Council Notable Trade Books in the Field of Social Studies list was starting. Biographies were being published in greater quantity than ever before, partly as a result of the social changes of the 1960s that brought the voices of minorities and women into public discourse, and partly as a result of educational funding that expanded the school market for children's books. The first Notable lists showed a large concentration of African-American titles, particularly books about slavery. Within a few years, a separate category was added for books about women.

At the same time, biography was becoming a field of great interest to critics and writers in both adult and children's literature. Periodicals and books about adult writing claimed, or rather reclaimed, biography as a form of literature. Articles appeared in the field of children's literature protesting the mediocre formula style of many children's biographies and demanding better research. Patrick Groff (1973) argued against the cut-and-paste work of many biographers who used secondary sources and borrowed from adult biographies, offering watered-down versions for young readers. Elizabeth Segal (1980) wittily exposed the falsity of a didactic biography of Beatrix Potter that turned the intelligent, creative, complex woman into a model of propriety and conventional goodness.

Meanwhile, reviewers were finding some extraordinary new works among the spate of biographies published in the early seventies. In the Notable list for 1973–74 appeared the names of two new authors who were to revolutionize biography for children: F. N. Monjo and Jean Fritz. Three books by Monjo appeared that year: *Grand Papa and Ellen Aroon* (1974), *Me and Willie and Pa* (1973), and *Poor Richard in France* (1973). In these books, three of the great figures of U.S. history—Thomas Jefferson, Abraham Lincoln, and Benjamin Franklin—are seen

in a new light, in simply told books for beginning readers, presented from the viewpoint of young children in their families. The wit and skill of Monjo's writing, based on careful research and authenticated facts, proved that biography could be scholarly and still be popular, readable, and short. Monjo (1976, 121) would later write that by using the clear-eyed realistic vision of childhood, he was trying to remove his famous subjects from their "remote, decaying pedestals" and make them into living people again.

In 1973, with the publication of *And Then What Happened, Paul Revere?*, Jean Fritz began her brilliant career in biographical writing. With humor, sympathetic understanding, and anecdotal history, Fritz made the dreary figures of early U.S. history into lively personalities who, despite human failings, accomplished great things. As Fritz (1976, 126) explained, she tried to surprise children with interesting facts that would "lend reality and life" to her subjects and capture the essence of their character. In her carefully researched books for young readers of every grade level, Fritz has accomplished a revolution in biographical writing, promoting the view that famous people should be seen not as models of virtue but as ordinary people who, because of special gifts or opportunity, accomplished extraordinary things.

As changes in biographical writing began to be recognized and appreciated, other authors explained and defended the genre. Milton Meltzer (1986), for example, spoke for the recognition of nonfiction and biographical writing as forms of literature. Milton Lomask (1986), author of numerous biographies for children, explained lucidly in his book *The Biographer's Craft* the step-by-step process by which he investigated a subject and recreated a life. Natlie S. Bober (1991) expressed her conviction that biography is made up of research and art in equal parts.

There is no question now, in the 1990s, that biography is a form of literature, subject to the same standards of writing as fiction, and the same standards of authenticity and research as the best nonfiction. When, in 1988, Russell Freedman's *Lincoln: A Photobiography* (1987) was awarded the Newbery Medal, it was a measure of the extent to which biography had won status in the world of children's lit-

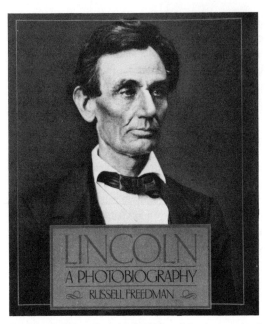

From *Lincoln: A Photobiography*, © 1987 Russell Freedman, reprinted by permission of Clarion Books.

erature. In his acceptance speech, Freedman (1988) claimed that biography had emerged from the servant's quarters of utility and had taken its place in the lofty "House of Literature."

Today, a wealth of biographies is available to teachers—biographies that are products of careful research, are interestingly written, and present a wider choice of subjects than ever before. The NCSS-CBC Notable lists provide a guide to titles recommended for quality of research, fine writing, good illustration, interesting contemporary and historical subjects, and innovative uses of biographical materials. Among the titles listed over the two decades in which they have been published, the Notable lists have identified and celebrated the trends and characteristics of the new and improved genre of juvenile biography. Some of the qualities that distinguish the new biography are the following.

Humor. Ever since Monjo and Fritz wrote their first biographies for younger readers in the early 1970s, wit and humor have been an established feature of biographical writing for children. Robert

Quackenbush's *Who Said There's No Man on the Moon?: A Story of Jules Verne* (1985) was selected for the 1985 list because it was lighthearted and embellished with witty cartoon-style illustrations.

New Voices, New Viewpoints. Autobiography, children's impressions, and reports from best friends or co-workers offer varied views of famous people. In *From the Door of the White House*, Preston Bruce (1984) offers fascinating insights into five presidential families from the perspective of the man who tended the White House door—Bruce himself.

Innovative Formats and Graphics. Picture book biographies and beautifully illustrated life stories can be found in abundance among the more recent titles published. Alice and Martin Provenson's *Leonardo da Vinci* (1984) set a new standard in pop-up books with its remarkable paper engineering. Leonard Everett Fisher produced dramatic black-and-white nonfiction picture books, among them *Prince Henry the Navigator* which was selected for the 1990 list. Diane Stanley's *Peter the Great* (1986) and *Shaka, King of the Zulus* (1988) are fine examples of illustrated biography.

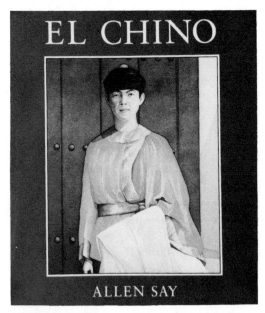

From *El Chino*, © 1990 Allen Say, reprinted by permission of Houghton Mifflin Company.

Wider Choice of Subjects. Many books now support and enhance themes of multiculturalism, diversity, and global education as they celebrate the lives of extraordinary individuals. Examples from the Notable lists include *El Chino* by Allen Say (1990) and *The Last Princess: The Story of Princess Ka'iulani of Hawai'i* by Fay Stanley (1991). *Arctic Explorer: The Story of Matthew Henson* by Jeri Ferris (1989) and *Quanah Parker,* the story of a Comanche war chief, by Len Hilts (1987) highlight the achievements of American minorities.

Contemporary Issues. Numerous biographies of sometimes controversial figures address current political and social concerns in books considered notable for their careful research and balanced approach. Recent biographies have been published about activists such as *Ché: Latin America's Legendary Guerilla Leader* by Anne Neimark (1989) and about crises of conscience, such as the Dreyfus case in *Captain of Innocence: France and the Dreyfus Affair* by Norman Finkelstein (1991).

Biographies that are chosen for their ability to interest young readers, as well as for the information presented, can play an important role in the literature-based curriculum. Whether a teacher chooses to develop discussion and activities around a central character in a book, or chooses to look for themes of justice, freedom, or other contemporary concerns, or whether it is some past age or culture that provides a focus for learning—the new biography fulfills all such needs and provides rich sources of material for the classroom.

References

Bober, Natlie S. "Writing Lives." *The Lion and the Unicorn* 15 (June 1991): 78–88.

Bruce, Preston. *From the Door of the White House.* New York: Lothrop, Lee and Shepard Books, 1984.

Daugherty, James. *Daniel Boone.* New York: Penguin USA, Viking, 1939.

Ferris, Jeri. *Arctic Explorer: The Story of Matthew Henson.* Minneapolis, Minn.: Carolrhoda Books, 1989.

Finkelstein, Norman. *Captain of Innocence: France and the Dreyfus Affair.* New York: G. P. Putnam's Sons, 1991.

Fisher, Leonard Everett. *Prince Henry the Navigator.* New York: Macmillan Publishing Co., 1990.

Freedman, Russell. New York: Clarion Books, 1987.

———. *Lincoln: A Photobiography.* "Newbery Medal Acceptance." *The Horn Book* 64 (July/August 1988): 444–51.

Fritz, Jean. *And Then What Happened, Paul Revere?* New York: Coward, McCann and Geoghegan, 1973.

———. "Making It Real." *Children's Literature in Education* 22 (Autumn 1976): 125–27.

Groff, Patrick. "Biography: The Bad or the Bountiful?" *Top of the News* 29 (April 1973): 210–17.

Hilts, Len. *Quanah Parker.* San Diego: Harcourt Brace Jovanovich, 1987.

Lomask, Milton. *The Biographer's Craft.* New York: Harper and Row, 1986.

Meltzer, Milton. "Notes on Biography." *Children's Literature Association Quarterly* 10 (Winter 1986): 172–75.

Monjo, F. N. *Me and Willie and Pa.* New York: Simon and Schuster, 1973.

———. *Poor Richard in France.* New York: Holt, Rinehart and Winston, 1973.

———. *Grand Papa and Ellen Aroon.* New York: Holt, Rinehart and Winston, 1974.

———. "Human Saints." *Children's Literature in Education* 22 (Autumn 1976): 121–24.

Neimark, Anne. *Ché: Latin America's Legendary Guerilla Leader.* Philadelphia: J. B. Lippincott Co., 1989.

Provenson, Alice, and Martin Provenson. *Leonard da Vinci.* New York: Penguin USA, Viking, 1984.

Quackenbush, Robert. *Who Said There's No Man on the Moon?: A Story of Jules Verne.* New York: Prentice-Hall, 1985.

Say, Allen. *El Chino.* Boston: Houghton Mifflin Co., 1990.

Segal, Elizabeth. "In Biography for Young Readers, Nothing Is Impossible." *The Lion and the Unicorn* 4 (Summer 1980): 4–13.

Stanley, Diane. *Peter the Great.* New York: Four Winds Press, 1986.

———. *Shaka, King of the Zulus.* New York: William Morrow and Co., 1988.

Stanley, Fay. *The Last Princess: The Story of Princess Ka'iulani of Hawai'i.* New York: Four Winds Press, 1991.

Weil, Ann. *Betsy Ross: Girl of Old Philadelphia.* Indianapolis, Ind.: Bobbs-Merrill, 1954.

Wibberley, Leonard. "The Land of the Ever Young." *The California Librarian* 23 (January 1962): 17–21.

Yates, Elizabeth. *Amos Fortune, Free Man.* New York: E. P. Dutton, 1950.

Chapter Five

The Treatment of War and Conflict in Young Adult Literature

Jack Zevin

Nothing could be smarter, more splendid, more brilliant, better drawn up than the two armies. Trumpets, fifes, hautboys, drums, cannons, formed a harmony such as has never been heard even in hell. The cannons first of all laid flat about six thousand men on each side; then the musketry removed from the best of worlds some nine or ten thousand blackguards who infested its surface.... Candide, who trembled like a philosopher hid himself as well as he could during this heroic butchery.

—from *Candide* by Voltaire

Several decades ago, it was unusual for children's books to address conflict in general, or wars in particular, and when they did so it was usually for patriotic purposes. The texts usually glossed over the less pleasant aspects of conflict or rendered armed conflict a rather colorful and glorious affair. As children's and young adult literature has grown into a mass field in its own right, a slow but noticeable increase has occurred in books that address conflicts of all eras through both fiction and nonfiction. In this chapter, I will analyze and draw conclusions about recent children's and young adult fiction and nonfiction that primarily address U.S. conflicts or world conflicts with direct connections to events that involved the United States. I will also offer suggestions about some ways fiction and nonfiction can be incorporated into learning programs.

Almost all of the works included in this review have appeared on the annual National Council for the Social Studies-Children's Book Council Notable Children's Trade Books in the Field of Social Studies lists between the years 1985 and 1990. The books collected for those lists have the advantage of public review

by a committee that was more critical and more reliable than single reviewers might have been in bringing works to judgment. Thus, it seems logical to argue that the quality of the works represented on the lists is high and that these books represent the best of what is available to teachers (and to the general public) for young people.

There is no shortage of children's books about conflict and the events preceding or following it. As one would expect, most of the books focus on famous events that occupy center stage in the history and social studies curriculum, e.g., the American Revolution, the Civil War, World War I, World War II, and the Vietnam War. With rare exception, most of the books discuss home events—those relevant to U.S. history—although a few describe conflicts in other times and places from either an insider or an outsider point of view. A foreign author occasionally appears in translation, but the vast majority of literature is generated by U.S. authors.

Most of the young adult and children's books are handsomely produced and include numerous photographs that enrich and enliven the text. Several of the Civil War books, particularly the nonfiction, offer excellent reproductions of the famous Matthew Brady battlefield photographs and the work of other artists and photographers. Surprisingly perhaps, authors have written books on conflict for almost every age level and often bring up sensitive issues for students to consider. Sometimes these issues and pictures are shocking and depressing, offering young people realistic images of the wars and rebellions they have either studied in their textbooks or heard about from parents and relatives. I see a tendency toward open and frank discussions of conflict across both the social scientific and literary volumes. This is a healthy development in an area that has frequently put a premium on masking the frightening aspects of wars, rebellions, and social conflict.

Some of the books are dull, but others are vibrant and involving; some are about people and tell their stories in personal terms whereas others describe events in a broad historical and political sweep. The authors' styles and messages vary considerably, ranging from dramatic to matter-of-fact stories, and from antiwar sentiments to vivid paeans to patriotic struggle. Teachers can use young adult and children's literature of this kind to raise questions about authors' perspectives and to build student consciousness not only of the events but of the ways in which writers use words to influence our mental images of what is happening. In the novel *Be Ever Hopeful, Hannalee* by Patricia Beatty (1988, 27–28), written from the viewpoint of a young Southern woman, the main characters, a brother and sister, have a discussion about Atlanta after the North's victory that one can only describe as evenhanded and conciliatory.

> I sighed. That was just like the Yankees to shoot at churches! I said "Our Confederate gunners wouldn't ever do that to a Yankee church."
>
> Again Davey laughed, "Don't you be so sure they never did. Our men wasn't so finicky on their way north to Gettysburg, Pennsylvania, back in '63. Now don't look like you don't believe me! What I tell you is true. There ain't no cause for you to be a fire-eater now, honey. The Yankees is here. Atlanta'll be full of 'em. They'll be thick as fleas on a bluetick hound's rump. The best thing to do is act so they don't take no notice of you. Don't give 'em any sass."

Leaving aside the issue of historical veracity, one feature of interest in this conversation is its commitment to a value of peacefulness. The young soldier Davey, who has lost an arm in the war, counsels his somewhat resentful younger sister to adjust to the new conditions, rather than to develop a sense of rage and revenge.

The book as a whole paints a picture of the post–Civil War South as a society ready and willing to rebuild their land in an atmosphere of reconciliation. I would argue that the novel is teaching young

people that even after conflicts with one's own people, peace and harmony can be achieved through new attitudes and a spirit of cooperation. Both sides are portrayed as engaging in cruel behavior such as destroying each others' churches. Other authors might not paint this type of portrait of the South after the Civil War or preach values in favor of conflict resolution through peaceful interaction. Teachers can bring out the central ideas of a selection by engaging students in discussion of an author's meaning and message especially as they affect the mind-set of the reader.

Purpose and Selection Criteria

By analyzing a range of children's and young adult works, I sought to determine if any pattern or trend emerged in the style and philosophy of books about conflict, and what overall "image" or message, if any, a sample of these works conveyed to their young readers. I chose books for this chapter that directly address wartime periods and scenes that either depict or discuss battles and violent upheaval, or their causes and consequences. At the very least, these books present details about events or personalities leading up to or devolving from one or more social conflicts or wars. Omitted were conflicts of a personal or familial nature unless these concerned national policies that led to, or emanated from, a period of hostile interaction between or within societies.

Analytic Categories

Conflicts, particularly the wars fought by a nation (and especially one's own), are loaded with historical meaning and are often difficult to discuss. The more contemporary the event, the greater the problem of an objective evaluation or judgment and the more likely bias, distortion, and political leanings will color the events. In analyzing each work individually, and the group as a whole, therefore, I was particularly interested in the ways authors present their views on war and which symbols and signs they choose to emphasize—e.g., the political or the social, the heroic or the mundane, the personal or the outside analyst. To organize my review, I looked at these works according to the following six dimensions:

- **Style.** Is it dramatic or matter-of-fact?
- **Story.** Is it told through the lives of ordinary people or famous leaders?
- **Voice.** Is it described from an insider perspective (personal) or an outsider perspective (impersonal)?
- **Sweep.** Is it discussed in largely political and historical terms or in social and cultural terms?
- **Moral.** Is it subjected to a clear judgment of right and wrong (pro or con) or narrated in non-judgmental, neutral words that avoid a position?
- **Philosophy.** Is the author making a statement that opposes war or evokes its horrors? Or is the author justifying the necessity of conflict, offering an image of heroism and glory to the battle scene?

Of the thirty-six books specifically about wars and conflicts that have appeared on the NCSS-CBC Notable lists over the last five years, a panel reviewed each in terms of the six dimensions described here.

Each title has been characterized as falling primarily into one of the six subdivisions—style, story, voice, sweep, moral, or philosophy—for the purposes of gathering a rough count of the ways children's authors approach the subject of war. The sample is assumed to be representative of quality literature rather than the totality of what is available to the public at all levels. To provide feedback and validation to the author, a panel of four reviewers—two pre-service graduate students and two practicing teachers—were asked to read a randomly selected subsample of the volumes considered in this paper. Their task was to decide if the six categories of analysis were distinct and reliable units for judging a book's character. Each of the four raters read and judged eight books resulting in a level of agreement calculated according to a Pearson's coefficient of interrater-reliability, as follows: style, .76; story, .93; voice, .89; sweep, .72; moral, .81; and philosophy, .67.

Also noted is the grade level of the work, using Children's Book Council categories for primary, intermediate, and advanced grades. These are, of course, rough estimates of the appropriate audience. Naturally, many of the works are far more sophisticated and complex than can be communicated by a simple six-category scheme of analysis. To discover fine

nuances and deeper meanings, each work should be read by a group of people who can debate both its literary and historical merits, as well as decide which messages, if any, dominate the narrative as a whole. Descriptive phrases are included in this bibliography with the invitation that you subject each selection to your own critical assessment of their approaches, value orientations, and quality.

It is often difficult to determine an author's intent and philosophy, particularly where deep and upsetting issues must be masked or toned down for consumption by young readers who the author wishes to reach emotionally and stimulate intellectually without frightening or propagandizing. For example,

From *The Boys' War*, © 1990 Jim Murphy, reprinted by permission of Clarion Books.

Jim Murphy, author of *The Boys' War* (1990), discusses the experiences of underage soldiers in the Civil War in descriptive terms without expressing any judgments about war itself. A typical passage about the adaptation of these youngsters to violent conflict notes that fighting a war changes any soldier, but it especially changed the boys who fought in the Civil War. When they had enlisted, they were naive, undisciplined, and used to doing farm-related chores. Given several months of drilling and experience in battle, these boys had turned into true soldiers. Granted they would never have the spit and polish to impress anyone while on parade, but their skill in the field had been honed to a killing edge. (36)

The author does not raise any questions about the morality of sending boys into battle, or what it means to be a "true" soldier at the age of eleven or twelve. Is he implying that good fighters are valuable at any age? Does he mean that minors who kill other soldiers—the enemy—are patriotic and therefore justified in their violent behavior? The author seems to savor their "skill in the field" that was "honed to a killing edge." This use of words seems to have a note of admiration that teachers and students might question. Just what message is the author trying to get across here? That a war of defense is justified? That minors should serve their country however violent the conflict? That war is romantic and inspiring? Or vile and psychologically damaging? An antiwar philosophy is obviously lacking here.

Survey Results ($N = 36$)

N	%		N	%	
Level			**Voice**		
6	17	Primary (K–2)	26	72	Personal (inside view of events)
11	31	Intermediate (3–6)	10	28	Impersonal (outside view of events)
19	53	Advanced (6–8)			
Topic			**Sweep**		
5	14	American Revolution	17	47	Political/Historical
8	22	Civil War	19	53	Social/Cultural
1	3	World War I			
10	28	World War II (including two works on the Lincoln Brigade in Spain)	**Moral**		
			26	72	Judgmental, Pro or Con
			10	28	Nonjudgmental, Avoids Positions
6	17	Vietnam War			
3	8	Alamo, Indian Wars, Overviews of U.S. Wars	**Philosophy on Conflict and Conflict Resolution**		
3	8	Other, Wars outside the United States	5	14	Antiwar (condemns all or most violence to achieve political goals and policies)
Style			11	31	Horrors of War (condemns both sides, but not war per se)
28	78	Dramatic	5	14	Neutral or Noncommittal (condemns neither side)
8	22	Matter-of-Fact	14	39	Justifies or Defends War (condemns mainly one side)
Story					
28	78	Ordinary People	1	3	Glorifies War, for Offense or Defense (condemns "other")
8	22	Great Leaders			

Rather, the excerpt reinforces a certain sense of drama and excitement about war and admiration for warriors.

It is passages like this that put the six categories I have proposed to the test. Decisions about which categories most appropriately characterize a given work must take into account the author's writing style and the tone as well as any overt expression of philosophy on war, warfare, or the causes of conflict. Therefore, judgments should be accepted as general rather than detailed and specific because a careful deconstruction of each work would make for an extremely lengthy analysis rather than a general survey of results.

Conclusions

Predictably, authors have written the majority of the children's and young adult books on this topic for an older audience, with an increasing percentage of the total rising as grade level increases. Slightly more than half of all the books over the five-year period are for the upper grades and middle school, but a significant number are available to younger children at the primary and intermediate levels.

The topics about which most of the children's and young adult books are written are skewed in favor of relatively few conflicts—especially the ever-popular American Revolution, Civil War, and World War II—with a growing number of works recently appearing on the struggle over Vietnam. The Civil War seems a perennial favorite of both authors and readers. Surprisingly perhaps, World War I received only one entry and only a smattering of work was devoted to all other wars in which the United States has been involved. This could be chance development, or perhaps authors feel that World War I is overworked or took place on battlefields remote for most young people. Several authors present stories of fighters and protesters who have taken part in unpopular or unofficial conflicts, seeking to bring new attention to episodes that have been either forgotten or underappreciated. For example, the two books (Katz and Crawford 1989; Lawson 1989) on the participation of Americans in the Lincoln Brigade, which fought on the side of the Republicans against the fascist-supported forces of Franco during the Spanish Civil War.

The vast bulk of the books examine wars and conflicts in which the United States was directly involved and do so largely from a U.S. point of view. Only four books offer students inside perspectives on wars in other lands that did not involve U.S. interests. Only two authors are foreign nationals whose writing was translated from another language into English. Thus, a minority of the total sample focuses on places and times outside the purview of U.S. historical development.

Most of the books, whether fiction or nonfiction, offer young people a dramatic retelling of events and convey events and personalities in an emotional tone designed to attract interest and develop empathy for characters. Matter-of-fact descriptions of events in dry historical tones or social scientific analysis are in a distinct minority (22 percent) as compared to journalistic or novelistic accounts (78 percent).

Corroborating the dramatic tone of most of the books about war and conflict, the vast majority are about ordinary people or are told through the eyes of characters who are witnesses to or participants in events rather than leaders or elite symbols. Stories are nearly all seen through the eyes of average citizens, draftees or volunteers, women and children (78 percent) and relatively few (22 percent) are about or told by the great heroes or heads of armies involved in wars and revolutions. This perhaps ties in with the trend toward social history that has achieved popularity among historians during the past two decades, and that fits in with authors' desires for sympathetic protagonists.

Furthermore, the vast bulk of the books (72 percent) are told in the first person or through a sympathetic character with whom young people can identify, rather than through neutral third-person accounts (28 percent) which tend to render events impersonal. Furthermore, authors portray many of the narrators, particularly in the fictional accounts, as young—usually teenagers or young adults. Even in most of the nonfiction histories or documentaries, common people representing main street, rather than sophisticated elites, are the focus of storytelling, offering firsthand witnesses to dramatic events.

Authors describe the sweep of events about equally from a historical or political perspective (47 percent) and from a social or cultural perspective (53 percent). About half of the books take mainly a political tack on events concentrating on the actions, policies, and issues that motivated the conflicts; the other half focuses particularly on social movements and the lives of people who witnessed or took part in the momentous conflicts of their times. The social or cultural works tend to stress economic and structural reasons for conflicts; the historically oriented works tend to stress political disagreements and governmental decisions.

Along with the dramatic and personal nature of about three-quarters of the volumes on war and conflict, most of the authors are unafraid of offering evaluations, whether for or against one side or the other, or in favor or opposed to certain policies of the governments involved. Some are willing to express their ideas in the plainest and most powerful terms for youngsters. In *Vietnam: Why We Fought—An Illustrated History*, for instance, Dorothy and Thomas Hoobler (1990, xi) present their judgment of the conflict in the book's introduction:

Vietnam was the most unpopular war in American history. It was the war in which Americans marched in the streets to oppose their own government. It was the "bad war," the war we lost. And that makes the pain of those who fought it, and those who visit the Wall, that much greater. Nothing anyone can say today can end that pain, but we can try to understand what caused it.

In effect, the authors argue that an immoral conflict is destructive both psychologically and physically, probably for both the victor and the vanquished, if those terms can be applied to a war that ends inconclusively. The strong words used and the lack of qualifiers immediately sets a tone of bluntness and discernment that will characterize the entire history of this struggle.

Teachers might discuss with students the authors' no-nonsense factual language as a guide to their overall philosophy, a portion of which they summarize in the concluding chapter:

What were the mistakes we made in Vietnam? The biggest error was in thinking that the United States was so powerful that it could achieve any goal. We had defeated the Nazis and the Japanese in World War II. Vietnam was a much smaller and weaker country. Most Americans thought we could certainly bend its people to our will. Even today, years after the end of the war, people still find the outcome difficult to swallow.

We did not realize that the Vietnamese were willing to take casualties and accept punishment that Americans would not. The Vietnamese had a cause—independence. The war was one more battle in their 2,000-year history of fighting foreign domination. To them it was worth their lives. (187)

Based on these passages, teachers could easily raise questions about the authors' general principles of foreign policy and their views of conflict as a means of settling disputes. We could ask students what the authors mean by accusing the United States of "thinking it was so powerful it could achieve any goal." Exactly what errors of judgment is the U.S. government being blamed for? Why do the authors portray the U.S. government as wanting to "bend" the Vietnamese to their view of politics? Is the tone of the passage bland and descriptive or angry and offended? How can you tell? Do the authors of this book have a full-fledged philosophy of human conflict? Can we decide from their standards what is a just or an unjust war? When a decision to fight is moral or immoral?

As you can see, just a few sentences from this book can stimulate discussion of important values and encourage young people to make some political decisions of their own. You might even call upon students to create human rights rules they can use to assess other books and reports they read or view, or to evaluate future conflict situations. A children's or young adult book with strong views and a powerful tone should assist in sparking student interest and promoting classroom debate.

Most of the books tend to focus on specific decisions by people, politicians, and generals, rather than general judgments about the causes, actions, or consequences of war as an instrument of human politics. For example, authors offer opinions about the wisdom of the South's strategy during the U.S. Civil War and the Johnson and Nixon administrations' decisions during the Vietnam conflict. Pro- and antigovernment judgments are about evenly divided among the twenty-six authors who venture opinions about the wars they describe. Few, however, are willing to make generalizations about the nature of conflict and conflict resolution.

Perhaps most interesting of all are authors' positions on the issue of conflict as a mode for settling disputes among and between peoples and nations. Only one author openly glorifies war and heroism on the battlefield. Just five authors take a stand against war itself, arguing that warfare is morally reprehensible what-

From *The Forty-Third War,* © 1989 Louise Moeri, reprinted by permission of Houghton Mifflin Company.

ever its object, defense or offense, whether victorious or in defeat. Only five authors adopt a neutral or noncommittal viewpoint on war, conflict, and violence, merely describing the chain of events without editorializing on motives or morals. Thus, those who either chose not to make a judgment or took the toughest positions, pro or con, account for only about one-third of the books. The largest proportion of the writers (70 percent) take the view that war is wrong and terrifying, but necessary for a wide variety of reasons. Some (39 percent) argue, in effect, that wars fought against aggressive or evil enemies can be justified on ethical grounds. Others (31 percent) describe wars as horrifying to both sides, but sometimes demanded by practical necessities of self-defense when all other diplomatic maneuvers and compromises fail. Almost no one endorses war as a noble or righteous policy that states and nations should turn to as the major instrument for solving conflicts. Nevertheless, only 14 percent of the writers for children take a position dead set against all wars as means for solving disputes. Quite clearly, a wide range of values toward war can be found in children's and young adult fiction and nonfiction with relatively few authors taking absolute positions. Most of the writers did choose, covertly or overtly, to communicate values to young people through dramatic, personal narrative, often seen from the vantage point of ordinary folk who express their judgments about the actors and actions taking place.

Opportunities for Teaching

Using children's and young adult fiction or nonfiction to supplement reading, writing, and social studies in elementary and middle schools can and should be part of every student's normal experience. The advantages for the teacher are many. First, both the readability and quality of the children's books are usually far superior to the textbooks we use in our classrooms. Second, through literature we offer young people the opportunity to immerse themselves fully in a time, place, event, or person—often from an insider perspective rather than from a broad, somewhat removed, overview. Third, the teacher has the potential to sharpen inferential and interpretational skills that students need to hone in order to understand authors' styles and messages. Your questions may, if you like, use the categories of analysis discussed in this essay: style, story, voice, sweep, moral, and philosophy. Or you can choose your own concepts from experience or other sources. Using a work of fiction or non-fiction as a base, you can develop interesting questions for classroom discussion or group inquiry. You could also prepare creative projects in which students write their own biographies, pen book reviews, or invent a story and characters to get across a message they want to promote. Inferential skills are crucial for success later on in school and in "real life," because the ability to read and interpret both words and images critically is part of daily survival in our complex, print- and media-oriented modern technological society.

Teachers who regularly engage students in recognizing writers' viewpoints and which values are central to their beliefs are providing a strong basis for critical reading. Furthermore, they may also spark or reinforce an interest in fiction, biography, and history through the process of working with children's and young adult literature as aids to finding and solving problems. As a result of the questions posed and issues identified, students should begin to ask about the effect writing and images have on their interpretations rather than simply accepting what is written or shown as always accurate and truthful. Creating an awareness of authors' styles, their manipulation of story and characters, choice of voice or perspective, and their overall moral and philosophical commitments provides students with tools for thinking that carry over into many fields of study in school and in daily life, from reading a newspaper account to watching a movie.

Books Assessed

P = Appropriate for primary grades (K–2)
I = Appropriate for intermediate grades (3–6)
A = Appropriate for advanced grades (6–8)
(These assessments should be viewed only as approximate.)

Beatty, Patricia. *Be Ever Hopeful, Hannalee*. New York: William Morrow and Co., 1988. (A) Civil War era.

_____. *Charley Skedaddle*. Mahwah, N.J.: Troll Associates, 1987. (I & A) Civil War era.

Berleth, Richard. *Samuel's Choice*. Niles, Ill.: Albert Whitman and Co., 1990. (I) American Revolution era.

Connolly, Peter. *Tiberius Claudius Maximus: The Cavalryman* and *Tiberius Claudius Maximus: The Legionary*. New York: Oxford University Press, 1989. (I) Roman Empire era.

Cosner, Sharon. *War Nurses*. New York: Walker and Co., 1988. (I & A) Overview: Civil War era through Vietnam conflict.

Frank, Rudolf. *No Hero for the Kaiser*. Translated from the German by Patricia Crampton. New York: Lothrop, Lee and Shepard Books, 1986. (A) World War I era.

Freedman, Russell. *Indian Chiefs*. New York: Holiday House, 1987. (I & A) Mostly focused on the nineteenth century.

Hamilton, Virginia. *Anthony Burns: The Defeat and Triumph of a Fugitive Slave*. New York: Alfred A. Knopf, 1988. (I & A) Pre–Civil War era.

Hiser, Berniece T. *Adventures of Charlie and His Wheat-Straw Hat: A Memorat*. New York: Dodd Mead, 1986. (P) Civil War era Appalachian story.

Hoobler, Dorothy, and Thomas Hoobler. *Vietnam: Why We Fought—An Illustrated History*. New York: Alfred A. Knopf, 1990. (I and A)

Hurwitz, Johann. *Anne Frank: A Life in Hiding*. Philadelphia: Jewish Publication Society, 1988. (I & A) World War II biography.

Katz, William Loren. *Black Indians: A Hidden Heritage*. New York: Macmillan Publishing Co., Atheneum Publishers, 1986. (I & A) Colonial era to Civil War.

Katz, William Loren, and Marc Crawford. *The Lincoln Brigade: A Picture History*. New York: Macmillan Publishing Co., Atheneum Publishers, 1989. (I & A) Spanish Civil War to beginning of World War II.

Lattimore, Deborah Nourse. *The Flame of Peace: A Tale of the Aztecs*. New York: HarperCollins Publishers, 1987. (P) Pre-Columbian story of enemy attack.

Lawson, Don. *An Album of the Vietnam War*. New York: Franklin Watts, 1986. (I & A) Causes and consequences of the Vietnam conflict.

_____. *The Abraham Lincoln Brigade: Americans*

Fighting Fascism in the Spanish Civil War. New York: Crowell, 1989. (I & A) Spanish Civil War and Pre–World War II era.

Lingard, Joan. *Tug of War.* New York: Penguin USA, Lodestar Books, 1990. (I & A) Story of Latvian family during World War II.

Longfellow, Henry Wadsworth. *Paul Revere's Ride.* New York: Penguin USA, Dutton Children's Books, 1989. (P) American Revolution era.

Marrin, Albert. *The War for Independence: The Story of the American Revolution.* New York: Macmillan Publishing Co., Atheneum Publishers, 1988. (A)

Matas, Carl. *Code Name Kris.* New York: Scribner/Scholastic, 1988. (A) Danish resistance story, World War II.

Mattingly, Christobel. *The Miracle Tree.* San Diego: Gulliver Books, 1985. (I) World War II era, bombing of Nagasaki.

Meltzer, Milton. *The American Revolutionaries: A History in Their Own Words 1750–1800.* New York: Crowell, 1987. (A) Firsthand accounts of the Revolutionary era.

_____. *Voices from the Civil War: A Documentary History of the Great American Conflict.* New York: Crowell, 1989. (I & A) Historical sources with background information.

Moeri, Louise. *The Forty-Third War.* Boston: Houghton Mifflin Co., 1989. (A) A 12-year-old child's experience with war in a Central American nation. (A)

Murphy, Jim. *The Boys' War.* New York: Clarion Books, 1990. (I) Accounts from underage soldiers in the Civil War.

Myers, Walter Dean. *Fallen Angels: A Vietnam Story.* New York: Scholastic, 1988. (A) Story of a 17-year-old boy at war in Vietnam.

Nelson, Theresa. *And One for All.* New York: Dell Publishing, 1989. (I) Story of a brother and sister in 1967.

Patent, Gregory. *Shanghai Passage.* New York: Clarion Books, 1990. (I & A) World War II as seen by a Jewish boy in Shanghai.

Ray, Deborah. *My Daddy Was a Soldier: A World War II Story.* New York: Holiday House, 1990. (P & I)

Ray, Delia. *A Nation Torn: The Story of How the Civil War Began.* New York: Penguin USA, Lodestar Books, 1990. (I & A) Factual recounting of the causes.

Roop, Peter, and Connie Roop. *Buttons for General Washington.* Minneapolis, Minn.: Carolrhoda Books, 1986. (P) Story of the American Revolution era.

Schur, Maxine. *Hannah Szenes: A Song of Light.* Philadelphia: Jewish Publication Society, 1986. (I & A) World War II Jewish hero biography.

Weidhorn, Manfred. *Robert E. Lee.* New York: Macmillan Publishing Co., Atheneum Publishers, 1988. (I & A) Biography of the Confederate general and leader.

Windrow, Martin. *The World War II GI.* New York: Franklin Watts, 1986. (I & A) Sweeping study of the life of the ordinary soldier.

Chapter Six
Talk Shows and Trade Books

Arlene F. Gallagher

The students walk quietly into the library, subdued by the presence of two video cameras. For weeks they have been preparing for this event by listening to their teacher read *Anthony Burns: The Defeat and Triumph of a Fugitive Slave* by Virginia Hamilton (1988). Several days ago, a poster appeared announcing that a talk show would be held in the library with two guests from the past: Anthony Burns and Richard Dana, the attorney who

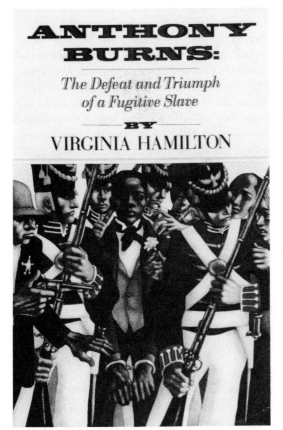

From *Anthony Burns: The Defeat and Triumph of a Fugitive Slave,* © 1988 Virginia Hamilton, reprinted by permission of Alfred A. Knopf.

defended Burns at his hearing in Boston. The students have agreed to a "willing suspension of disbelief" for an hour so that they can question these two men about their lives, their work, and the hardships they endured.

These students, normally the "cool dudes" in their school, are surprisingly a bit nervous. They have their questions written on three-by-five cards but most of them will try to speak from memory rather than referring to their notes. They settle into their seats and the talk show begins as the host sets the stage with some background information.

The activity that follows uses one book, Hamilton's *Anthony Burns.* Many other titles, cited in the bibliography, could serve as the basis for talk shows, or teachers could use several books on one individual or topic. One class even invited a horse to be interviewed, using *Black Beauty* as the basic text. The talk-show technique demonstrates the power of literature. Furthermore, the talk show format is engaging because everyone has a part to play and yet the approach does not demand elaborate preparation or scripts to memorize. Simply choose a topic or an individual to study, provide the background information through books or other resources, select the guests, and set a date for the event. It can be elaborate or simple, depending on students' age and research ability.

Background on Anthony Burns

In 1854, Anthony Burns escaped to Boston, where he was arrested on a false charge of theft so that his owner could claim him as property. Although Burns was defended by able counsel, he was returned to his owner and marched through the streets of Boston under federal guard to the chanting of "Shame! Shame!" by thousands who opposed the decision. He was returned to Richmond, Virginia, where he spent four months in jail in handcuffs and leg irons. He never completely recovered his health from that experience. Eventually his freedom was bought and he accepted a generous scholarship offered by a Boston woman to attend Oberlin College in Ohio. In 1856, Charles Emery Stevens wrote Burns's biography, *Anthony Burns: A History*, and much of the profit went to further Burns's education.

The hearings in 1854 were controversial primarily because abolitionist feelings were running high in Boston. A number of influential people had spoken out against slavery and the Fugitive Slave Act, a federal law that allowed owners to reclaim escaped slaves by presenting proof of ownership. Hamilton's book recreates the reality of slavery in the same way that Harriet Beecher Stowe's *Uncle Tom's Cabin*, published just two years prior to Burns's capture, influenced public sentiment about slavery.

The following activity is set forth in considerable detail to provide a comprehensive model for the reader. Preparation does not need to be this extensive.

Introduction by the Talk Show Host

"Today's talk show has some unusual features that you haven't seen on Oprah Winfrey or Phil Donahue's shows. As you know, the guests are from the past and we have set the time at seven years after Anthony Burns's ordeal in Boston. The year is now 1861 and Burns, having achieved his freedom, has become a minister. You will address him as Reverend Burns during this show. Our other guest is Richard Dana, the lawyer who stepped forward and offered to defend Anthony Burns without charge. Dana was already well-known as the author of *Two Years before the Mast*, a book that revealed the cruelty visited upon sailors and called for their just and humane treatment.

"It is important that, as members of the audience, you have some knowledge of the times. Antislavery feeling was at a fevered pitch in the North and the Burns case rocked Boston.

"Anthony Burns had escaped from Virginia to Boston, where he lived and worked as a free person for a few short months. He was arrested and accused of stealing jewelry and taken to the Boston courthouse.

There he was confronted by Charles Suttle, his owner. When Suttle asked why he ran away, Burns claimed that he fell asleep on a ship where he was working and the ship set sail. Burns's acknowledgment of Suttle was a key element in proving that Burns was, in fact, the runaway slave in question.

"The week that Burns was arrested was anniversary week for abolitionists in Boston. Both those against slavery and those seeking the vote for women were holding a convention. The arrest captured the attention of all the people attending the convention.

"During today's talk show, you will be able to ask any questions you wish of the two guests. We will be using a 'freeze technique' so that we can put our guests into a state of suspended animation if I, or any of you, want to talk in the present for any reason.

"And now let me introduce the two guests, Reverend Anthony Burns and counselor Richard Dana."

And so began a return to 1861 for an hour in a school library during which students asked questions of the two men from the past. They had been warned ahead of time that if they recognized the guests they were to keep their promise of a willing suspension of disbelief and pretend that the two guests were Burns and Dana reincarnated. At the end of the show, the guests were introduced as themselves so that students could discuss the experience with them. Anthony Burns was played by their school principal, Nanzetta Merriman. Merriman dressed in black that day and played his role with a calm and serious demeanor. Richard Dana was played by Steven Coren, a practicing attorney in Massachusetts. Both of these men were pleased, even flattered, to be invited to participate, and talked with students at length about how they prepared themselves and how it felt to play their roles.

Teachers often have students pretend to be characters from books to do role-plays, journal writing, or class presentations. A talk show format has the advantage of involving all students and using other resource people. The activity can easily be undertaken without using additional people, but the resource person seems to add a special dimension.

Resource People in Classrooms

The use of resource people in social studies classes has been found to be one of the most memorable experiences that students have from their elementary years. In some fields of study, such as citizenship or law-related education, the use of a resource person has been identified as one of the *key* ingredients for a successful program. Although it takes some preparation and organization by the classroom teacher, the resource person offers benefits that far outweigh the extra effort. Senior citizens, for example, have a wealth of information because many of them have lived the history your students are studying. Teachers are often surprised at how willing people are to come to their classrooms.

Preparing for the Talk Show

The host needs to become familiar with the background of the guests. In this case, a careful reading and rereading of Virginia Hamilton's book, a review of the historical time period, and a review of the geographical locations was enough. The teacher, a student, or a parent can play the role of host. Or, there could be more than one host.

The guests prepared themselves by reading Hamilton's book and thinking about the character they were going to play. They were also invited to suggest specific questions that might be asked.

The students prepared themselves by listening to Hamilton's book read aloud and by determining appropriate questions. This took about two weeks worth of social studies classes to accomplish. In other classes, students prepared for the event in a variety of ways, such as working in small groups and reading independently.

Social Studies Application: History

It is helpful to display a simplified time line of the major events of this period so that students can understand the context of Anthony Burns's capture. Most U.S. history textbooks contain time lines that you can modify for this purpose.

The rift between the North and the South was growing wider and wider during this time. Much of the disagreement focused on the slavery issue.

Antislavery feeling in the North had grown rapidly since 1851 when another slave, Thomas Sims, was captured and returned to slavery. At that time, five hundred business and professional men in Boston volunteered as special constables to aid the marshal in removing the prisoner from the city. Public sentiment had changed markedly in three years. Some historians believe that the publication of Harriet Beecher Stowe's *Uncle Tom's Cabin* in 1852 was significant in creating sympathy for the plight of slaves.

Not all, however, were sympathetic to the condition of slavery. President Franklin Pierce was proslavery and supported the Fugitive Slave Act, which provided that a runaway slave captured in any free state must be returned its owner. According to the procedure, a U.S. Commissioner would issue a fugitive slave warrant and receive ten dollars if it resulted in conviction but only five dollars if the slave were acquitted. In the case of Anthony Burns, Judge Loring was also the U.S. Commissioner.

The Fugitive Slave Act was a part of the Compromise of 1850, which attempted to settle the differences between the North and the South. Pertinent selections from this complicated piece of legislation are included in Virginia Hamilton's book.

Social Studies Application: Geography

Many important geographic connections can be made during this activity. Maps of the United States then and now will help students locate the events. Especially note Virginia and Massachusetts and the sea route that Burns probably took to escape to Boston. A detailed map of Massachusetts and a discussion of the kind of transportation available will help students appreciate how difficult it was for Burns to receive news and to travel to Boston for the abolitionist convention and the trial. The Missouri Compromise also played a key role in the events—a map showing which states allowed slavery would be useful.

Geography is an integral aspect of Anthony Burns's story. It was, in fact, Anthony Burns's location that affected his life so dramatically. Slaves were confined to specific geographic areas and states were identified as either free or not free. Many debates were held concerning whether a particular state should remain a slave state and whether a state should be admitted to the union as a slave state or as a free state.

Prepared Questions

The following questions can serve as examples for students. Students should, however, generate their own. These might be used to get started.

You might break the class up into small groups and have each group focus on one aspect of Burns's life: his early years, his experience at the Hiring Ground, his relationship with his family, or his experience in jail, for example.

Questions for Anthony Burns

- In general, how did a slave owner name slaves?
- You were not named in the same way as most slaves. Do you know why?
- Do you know who your father was?
- What was your mother like?
- How would you describe the place called the Hiring Ground where slaves were brought to be sold and rented?
- How were slaves examined by prospective buyers?
- Although some slave owners treated their slaves humanely, many did not. What was it like to work for Mr. and Mrs. Foote?
- You have noticed that Reverend Burns does not move his right hand. What was the "accident" that caused the injury to your hand?
- Although it was against the law for slaves to learn to read, you learned. How?
- Although many slaves ran away, many more did not. Slaves were not watched or guarded all of the time. Why didn't more slaves run away?
- Can you tell us how you were treated at first by the guards and then what you think motivated them to chip in money to buy you a new suit?
- You were kept in a trader's jail in Richmond, Virginia, for four months. Can you describe that experience?
- How did you finally become free?

Questions for Richard Dana

- What was it like living in Boston in the 1850s? Were most people in Boston for or against slavery?

- You wrote *Two Years before the Mast,* a book about traveling at sea, but you are a lawyer not a writer. Why did you write the book?
- What was it about your book that made it so successful?
- Why did you volunteer to defend Anthony Burns?
- Had you ever defended a fugitive slave before? What was the result?
- The Fugitive Slave Act was part of the Compromise of 1850. What did this mean?
- What had to be proved to enforce the Fugitive Slave Act?
- Who presided at Burns's hearing? Did you think this person was fair? Why or why not?
- A Massachusetts law forbade state officials from returning former slaves to slavery. Wasn't the hearing against the law?
- Do you think Commissioner Loring should have resigned his position rather than preside at this hearing, which could return a free man to slavery?
- No television or radio existed in those days and newspapers were not as available as they are today. Many people came to the hearings and to Boston when Anthony Burns was to be returned. How did people know that these events were happening? (Whoever asks this question may have to explain the concept of television to the guests. Or the host can "freeze" the guests and discuss another way to ask the question.)
- Do you think it would have made a difference in the outcome of the trial if television had been available for daily coverage of the event?
- Some people tried to buy Anthony Burns so that they could set him free. Do you think this was something people who were opposed to buying and selling human beings as property should do?
- Why weren't people able to buy Reverend Burns?
- Can you tell us how you were treated by the marshal and his personnel in the courthouse and whether you think that treatment had an influence on the outcome of the trial?
- Did President Franklin Pierce have any influence on what happened to Anthony Burns?
- As you look back on the trial, what might you have done differently that might have helped you win the case?

Expanding the Guest List

Keep in mind that it is not only the central character that makes an interesting guest for a show. Those people who were close to the individual, or even those who knew the person slightly, can offer various perspectives. Some research about the time period will suggest other figures who your students might like to interview. For example, in the Anthony Burns show the following people could be guests:

- Mr. and Mrs. Foote—slave owners who rented Anthony Burns from his owner.
- Benjamin F. Hallett—United States District Attorney.
- Edward Greeley Loring—Judge of Probate, Commissioner for taking bail and affidavits, presiding over slave cases.
- Edward G. Parker—lawyer for Charles Suttle.
- Franklin Pierce—fourteenth U.S. president, from 1853 to 1857.
- Charles F. Suttle—Colonel in Virginia Militia, owner of Anthony Burns.
- Big Walker—Possibly Anthony Burns's father; driver (representative) of Charles Suttle's slaves.

Other Notable Books for Talk Shows

Biographies and autobiographies generally lend themselves best to a talk show activity, although any historical novel will work well. The letters at the end of each annotation indicate the book's grade level: P = Primary, I = Intermediate, A = Advanced. These levels are general guidelines only and are not meant to be prescriptive.

Anderson, Joan. *1787*. Illustrated by Alexander Farquharson. New York: Harcourt Brace Jovanovich, 1987. (I & A) This blend of fact and fiction is set in Philadelphia during the summer that the U.S. Constitution was written. The events are seen through the eyes of James Madison but many other key figures appear. Includes the text of the Constitution.

Ashabranner, Brent. *Always to Remember: The Story of the Vietnam Veterans Memorial*. Photographs by Jennifer Ashabranner. New York: Dodd Mead, 1988. (I & A) This photo essay tells of the crusade of Jan C. Scruggs, the Vietnam veteran who spearheaded the drive for the memorial, and of Maya Ying Lin, the architectural student whose design was chosen.

Blumberg, Rhoda. *The Incredible Journey of Lewis and Clark*. New York: Lothrop, Lee and Shepard Books, 1987. (I & A) This comprehensive chronicle of the heroic adventures inspired by President Thomas Jefferson's vision of a bicoastal United States is heavily illustrated with maps, prints, and photographs. Lewis and Clark were the first to document the people, plants, animals, and geography of the land west of the Mississippi River.

Faber, Doris, and Harold Faber. *We the People: The Story of the United States Constitution Since 1787*. New York: Charles Scribner's Sons, 1987. (A) This historical survey, illustrated with prints and photographs, begins with the Constitutional Convention and discusses the U.S. Constitution as a living, changing document. An anecdotal approach to politicians and the climates that surrounded the ratification of the twenty-six amendments will help readers appreciate the Constitution (which is included).

Freedman, Russell. *Lincoln: A Photobiography*. New York: Clarion Books, 1987. (I & A) This book includes many photographs, prints, and reprints of original documents along with an absorbing look at Lincoln's career. Original writings and a list of Lincoln memorials is included.

Fritz, Jean. *The Great Little Madison*. New York: G. P. Putnam's Sons, 1989. (I & A) Jean Fritz has written so many outstanding books that it was difficult to choose one. Because Madison is such a key figure in U.S. history, this book will be useful to many teachers and students. Delving into Madison's personal relationships as deeply as his political achievements, Fritz addresses Madison's clashes with Patrick Henry, his romance with Dolley Pane Todd, and his friendship with Thomas Jefferson. A talk show with these three additional guests would be dynamic.

Hamilton, Virginia. *Anthony Burns: The Defeat and Triumph of a Fugitive Slave*. New York: Alfred A. Knopf, 1988. (I & A) This is an extensively researched biography of the slave who escaped to Boston in 1854. Burns's owner instigated his arrest and prevailed at the trial that caused a furor between abolitionists and those who were determined to enforce the Fugitive Slave Act. The author alternates chapters between the time of the trial and Burns's childhood.

Lindbergh, Reeve. *Johnny Appleseed*. Illustrated by Kathy Jacobsen. Boston: Little, Brown and Co., 1990. (P & I) This biographical poem and details of folk art tell the story of John Chapman (1774–1845), a naturalist and missionary who distributed apple trees and seeds from his nursery to settlers of the American frontier. The book includes a historical note.

Meltzer, Milton. *Columbus and the World around Him.* New York: Franklin Watts, 1990. (A) Meltzer, a distinguished author and biographer, has written more than seventy books. Many of them would serve well as talk show material. This story of the Italian adventurer illuminates the European culture of Columbus and shows how it shaped Columbus's thinking and his burning desire for riches, power, and fame.

Stanley, Diane, and Peter Vennema. *Good Queen Bess: The Story of Elizabeth I of England.* Illustrated by Diane Stanley. New York: Four Winds Press, 1990. (I) A biography of the strong-willed queen who ruled for forty-five years. The detailed color illustrations show the dress, customs, and decor of Elizabethan times.

Weiss, Ann E. *The Supreme Court.* Hillside, N.J.: Enslow Publishers, 1987. (A) The United States Supreme Court and its justices are examined through famous cases and issues in particular eras of its history.

Chapter Seven

Using Literature Sets to Promote Conversation about Social Studies Topics

Myra Zarnowski

High-quality children's trade books provide teachers with exciting possibilities for teaching social studies. In fact, they offer a means of overcoming one of the most nagging problems associated with textbook-driven programs: brief and simple explanations of complex topics.

Instead of a single perspective on a topic, trade books offer multiple perspectives. They show children that an event or an idea can be interpreted many ways. Instead of short, superficial accounts, trade books enable children to slow down and explore topics in depth. Subjects that are reduced to a page, a paragraph, or even a single line in a textbook can be the focus of several books. Trade books like those on the National Council for the Social Studies-Children's Book Council's Notable Children's Trade Books in the Field of Social Studies lists are written with both intelligence and feeling. Children can respond to these books with their minds and their hearts, taking in facts while acknowledging their emotions.

The possibilities for using trade books come with sobering challenges for classroom teachers. Even under the best circumstances—a classroom with a sizable collection of excellent books and eager readers—basic questions still remain: How can we use these books to help us meet our goals as social studies educators? How can we encourage children to examine critically the material they read? How can we involve children in deep investigations of social issues and then help them apply their knowledge beyond the classroom?

This chapter reviews one simple yet powerful means of introducing literature into social studies programs: the use of literature sets. Literature sets are collections of approximately five to fifteen books that are related in some way. A literature set can consist of books on a single topic, books by a single author, or books from a single genre.

Literature sets provide children with interesting material to think about, discuss, and apply. Once the sets are assembled, children work in small groups to read, make connections across various titles, and share their responses with others (Harste, Short, and Burke 1988; Hanssen, Harste, and Short 1990; Heine 1991). Such a procedure provides a foundation for thinking about social issues. It can also foster concept development, especially when children encounter and reencounter a concept in several books (Hanssen 1990).

The section that follows describes how literature sets were used in one 6th grade classroom. The sets, drawn from the 1985–90 NCSS-CBC Notable lists address important social issues of our time: poverty, human rights, immigration, the environment, and civil rights. The following is an example of how a teacher can introduce a large number of books in a classroom in a manageable and purposeful manner.

Literature Sets in the Classroom: A Lived-Through Experience

The setting for this project was Lila Alexander's 6th grade classroom at P.S. 201 in Flushing, Queens. Like most New York City classes, the student population is ethnically diverse, with a lively mix of backgrounds, viewpoints, and concerns. I joined Lila's class approximately three times per week over the course of several months to watch, record, and participate in their use of literature sets in the social studies program.

Our goal was to bring together groups of children to examine and explore their views through reading, writing, and conversation as a basic step toward civic awareness and civic participation. Like Ernest Boyer (1991, xvi), Lila and I believe that "citizenship training, if it means anything at all, means teaching students to think critically, listen with discernment, and communicate with power and precision." To work toward these ends, we followed a series of cumulative steps.

Step 1: Creating the Literature Sets and Introducing the Books

The literature sets Lila and I put together (see reference section) addressed five current issues that we thought children would find relevant to their lives: poverty, human rights, immigration, the environment, and civil rights. Each literature set provided a rich assortment of material and often included a number of formats and genres—picture books, photo essays, full-length novels, and informational books. The set of books on the environment, for example, included the picture book *Just a Dream* (Van Allsburg 1990), the photo essay

From *Just a Dream*, © 1990 Chris van Allsburg, reprinted by permission of Houghton Mifflin Company.

Riverkeeper (Ancona 1990), and the fact-filled adventure story *One Day in the Tropical Rain Forest* (George 1990). The set on human rights included the informational book *The Bill of Rights:*

How We Got It and What It Means (Meltzer 1990), as well as several realistic novels such as *The Gold Cadillac* (Taylor 1987), *Mississippi Bridge* (Taylor 1990), and *The Road to Memphis* (Taylor 1990) that detail the experiences of people who were denied their basic rights. We hoped that this varied collection of material would spark conversation and provide many opportunities for comparisons and contrasts.

Although we began with these specific literature sets, we used them flexibly, adding titles from the school and local libraries when it became clear that children were interested in certain issues related to their topics. This happened, for example, when the group studying poverty focused their reading and discussion on the problems of the homeless. Another way that literature sets grew was when group members brought in related newspaper articles. The group studying immigration, for example, found articles about Russian immigrants in Israel and Haitian refugees in the United States.

We introduced each literature set to the students before they were asked to join a group delving into that set. Either Lila or I briefly discussed a number of the titles from each set, highlighting such things as the setting of the book (time and place), memorable incidents, real people or imaginary characters, and questions that the book might answer for a reader. These introductions were brief, lasting approximately ten minutes per set, but served to generate interest among the children and provide them with a basis for selecting study groups and reading material.

Step 2: Group Discussions about Social Issues

Lila divided her class of twenty-five students into groups of five, each group studying one literature set. She formed these groups on the basis of the children's preferences. It was our hope that these small groups would allow every child many opportunities to speak and to listen to others. She told the children that they would meet in their groups several times per week to discuss their topic, and they were given time to prepare.

Preparation consisted of two basic activities. First, the children spent time each day reading books from their literature sets. Second, they kept journals in which they recorded interesting information and their thoughts about this information. In this way, we encouraged them to take a "facts-and-feelings" approach to their reading (Zarnowski 1990).

Group discussions frequently began with one child sharing a journal entry. These entries often included questions, thoughts, or interesting pieces of information. For example, by sharing the following excerpt with her group, one girl was able to bring up both the source of her confusion as a reader and her concerns as a world citizen:

> This book is about the greenhouse effect, carbon dioxide and stuff like that. It tells you what could happen if we don't stop [producing] acid rain, using energy, polluting the air, and burning trees. I don't understand what global warming means. I thought it was *global warming*. The book doesn't tell. This book makes me feel kind of scared of what's going to happen to the world.

This journal entry enabled the group studying the environment to begin to clarify their understanding of their topic. They did this by learning the words they needed to discuss the topic and by raising personal concerns.

Lila and I also prepared for these discussions by reading as many books as possible and by writing our own journal entries. As we read, we focused our attention on the possibilities for helping children deepen their understanding of social science content. To do this, we framed the following series of questions that we referred to during and after our reading so that we could seize "teachable moments" as they occurred during discussions.

History
- What events are described?
- Are these events described as having multiple causes and effects? What are they?
- How do these events influence current events?
- What things have changed since the events described occurred?
- What things have remained the same?

Geography
- What locations are described? How?
- Are accounts of how people have changed the earth included?
- Are accounts of how the earth's features have affected people's lives included?

Economics
- Are accounts of how people address the problem of scarcity included?
- What economic goals are described? Problems? Solutions? Successes or failures?

Civics
- Are people shown as concerned and active citizens?
- What kinds of decisions do they make?
- What kinds of actions do they take?
- What rights do they have as citizens? What responsibilities?

Anthropology
- What culture or cultures are described? How?
- How was this information learned?
- Has a particular culture changed over time? How? Rapidly? Slowly?

Sociology
- Are groups shown as belonging to a variety of groups? Which ones?
- What do these groups accomplish? How?

This self-questioning technique, originally developed to help teachers focus their attention on the literary elements while preparing to share novels with children (Eeds and Peterson 1991), was equally useful to us as a means of focusing our attention on social science content. Using these questions, we became aware of the possibility of looking at poverty from a historical perspective; for example, we noted that several of the books referred to poverty during the Depression and that we could compare conditions then and now. We also noted that the books on the environment would enable us to discuss how citizens enact new laws that respond to their concerns. Our questions opened up to us many possibilities for building on the children's comments.

During group discussions, Lila and I encouraged the children to share their responses to the material, make connections among the books they were reading, and raise additional questions for further research and reading. As active participants, we moved in and out of the various groups, sharing our responses, providing relevant information, and raising questions we thought would challenge our students.

One conversation that occurred early in the project shows the active role Lila played in focusing children's attention on finding themes within the material:

Paula: I was reading about the Irish. If America is the land of freedom, why are immigrants treated so badly?

Bruce: They don't shoot them.

Lila: Paula's point was that they were badly treated.

Ellen: The same thing happened to the Chinese.

John: The West Indians—it was the same.

Lila: Is there a pattern here?

During the discussion that followed, several children offered examples of how immigrants were treated. One student took the opportunity to think out loud. She raised her own question, and after pausing to allow another child to speak, suggested several possible answers:

Ellen: When people come here, they want to make things better. Some find conditions are worse. Why don't they leave?

David: They *would* be sent back if they were sick.

Ellen: They might get into trouble if they returned. They might not want to return. They might not have enough money to return.

Discussions such as these occurred for several weeks and enabled the children to clarify their ideas, raise questions, share information, and practice sustained conversation. They gained familiarity with their topics, which enabled them to comment on these topics with confidence.

Step 3: Sharing beyond the Classroom Community

One of the major goals of social studies instruction is preparing students to be citizens who are involved in the issues of their time. Lila and I saw our project as one modest step toward helping her students become informed about several pressing contemporary topics. Once they were informed, they would be ready to engage in dialogue beyond the usual confines of the classroom. We wanted these children to voice their opinions to other interested children and adults, including parents and community leaders.

To enter this broader conversational community, we needed to create something to share that would also promote further dialogue. Lila and I decided to engage the children in writing personal essays.

The personal essay was particularly appropriate for us because it is a forum for exploring ideas in a tentative, open-ended way. We decided to reclaim the original, less-structured, exploratory conception of the essay—instead of the traditional five-paragraph school essay—so that we could encourage students to share their thoughts and take at least a tentative stance on a current issue (Newkirk 1989). To do this, we asked the children to reread their journals, think about their past conversations, and then write about what was *on their minds* when they thought about their literature set topic.

At the same time, Lila and I introduced the children to the op-ed page of the newspaper. We shared several pieces that we believed would be accessible if we provided the necessary background information. We also noted and referred frequently to columnist A. M. Rosenthal's feature "On My Mind" in the *New York Times* because this title and many of Rosenthal's columns captured for us the personal involvement and reflection required in preparing an essay.

In time, each child produced an essay related to some facet of the literature set studied. We then assembled these essays into five "editorial pages," one for each of the literature set topics. The following excerpt shows the combined influence of reading and conversation on one child's writing.

The Very Typical American Family

Let's take a typical American family. A nice house—not too extravagant but good enough—a new Volvo, new clean furniture. Father works on computers in an office. Mother stays home with younger kids and waits for older kids to return from school.

One day father gets laid off from work. Rent, money, food, and health checkups are quickly due for some attention. Rent isn't paid. Their house is lost. The typical American family is now on the streets, waiting on the breadline every so often. It's as fast as that. A book I've read, *Poverty in America* by Milton Meltzer (1986), has given me some things to think about, such as the problem I just gave as an example. It's like a dynamite stick lit by the economy and politics.

Some people consider the homeless crazy or sick, but that's not true for most homeless people. They're just denied common resources. People who help the homeless claim the poor are poor because they lack not just an income but legal services, public amenities, basic human respect, and so on. They are deprived of ordinary activities in everyday life. They can't take a vacation, can't eat a meal in a restaurant, or give their children a birthday party.

Our homeless population is increasing rapidly. Poverty, the way I and others see it, is not an income level but a way of life. The world is breaking down slowly, and if there are no more people left to help it, besides the leaders who obviously don't care one way or another, the world will just keep on getting worse. "We the people," our leaders said; I think they've forgotten what that means. They need to focus more on why they're here and not so much on being popular.

This essay and others like it provided us with a vehicle for extending children's dialogue to members of our neighborhood community who later joined the class to respond to their editorials. The children were ready for this conversation because they had an idea of where they stood on at least one complex issue of our time.

Other Literature Set Possibilities

Although this chapter describes one class's experience using literature sets, the idea can be used flexibly. Beginning with the NCSS-CBC Notable list, teachers can develop their own literature sets. Sets can correspond to social studies curriculum objectives, student interests, current events, or holidays and other dates of significance.

Children can also respond to the books they read in a number of ways. As they move from reading and small-group conversation to sharing their ideas with larger groups, children can express themselves through art, drama, and music as well as writing. These activities—which follow logically from the fundamental experience of reading good books and having conversations—reveal the complex, intriguing nature of social studies.

References

Boyer, Ernest L. Foreword to *Civitas: A Framework for Civic Education,* NCSS Bulletin no. 86, edited by Charles F. Bahmueller. Calabasas, Calif.: Center for Civic Education, 1991.

Eeds, Maryann, and Ralph Peterson. "Teacher as Curator: Learning to Talk about Literature." *The Reading Teacher* 45 (October 1991): 118–26.

Hanssen, Evelyn. "Planning for Literature Circles: Variations in Focus and Structure." In *Talking about Books: Creating Literate Communities,* edited by Kathy G. Short and Kathryn M. Pierce. Portsmouth, N.H.: Heinemann Educational Books, 1990.

Hanssen, Evelyn, Jerome C. Harste, and Kathy Short. "In Conversation: Theory and Instruction." In *Beyond Communication: Reading Comprehension and Criticism,* edited by Deanne Bogdan and Stanley B. Straw. Portsmouth, N.H.: Boynton/Cook Publishers, 1990.

Harste, Jerome C., Kathy G. Short, and Carolyn Burke. *Creating Classrooms for Authors.* Portsmouth, N.H.: Heinemann Educational Books, 1988.

Heine, Patricia. "The Power of Related Books." *The Reading Teacher* 45 (September 1991): 75–77.

Newkirk, Thomas. *Critical Thinking and Writing: Reclaiming the Essay.* Urbana, Ill.: National Council of Teachers of English, 1989.

Zarnowski, Myra. *Learning about Biographies: A Reading and Writing Approach for Children.* Washington, D.C.: National Council for the Social Studies and National Council of Teachers of English, 1990.

Literature Sets for Children

The Environment

Ancona, George. *Turtle Watch.* New York: Macmillan Publishing Co., 1987.

_____. *Riverkeeper*. New York: Macmillan Publishing Co., 1990.

Elkington, John, Julia Hailes, Douglas Hill, and Joel Makower. *Going Green: A Kid's Handbook to Saving the Planet*. New York: Penguin USA, Puffin Books, 1990.

Elting, Mary. *Volcanoes and Earthquakes*. New York: Simon and Schuster, 1990.

George, Jean Craighead. *One Day in the Tropical Rain Forest*. New York: HarperCollins Publishers, 1990.

Huff, Barbara A. *Greening the City Streets: The Story of Community Gardens*. New York: Clarion Books, 1990.

Lauber, Patricia. *Seeing Earth from Space*. New York: Orchard Books, 1990.

Patent, Dorothy Hinshaw. *Yellowstone Fires: Flames and Rebirth*. New York: Holiday House, 1990.

Pringle, Laurence. *Restoring Our Earth*. Hillside, N.J.: Enslow Publishers, 1987.

Van Allsburg, Chris. *Just a Dream*. Boston: Houghton Mifflin Co., 1990.

Poverty

Ashabranner, Brent. *Dark Harvest: Migrant Farmworkers in America*. New York: Dodd Mead, 1985.

Bess, Clayton. *Tracks*. Boston: Houghton Mifflin Co., 1986.

Branscum, Robbie. *The Girl*. New York: HarperCollins Publishers, 1986.

Grove, Vicki. *Good-Bye, My Wishing Star*. New York: G. P. Putnam's Sons, 1988.

Locker, Thomas. *Family Farm*. New York: Penguin USA, Dial Books for Young Readers, 1988.

Meltzer, Milton. *Poverty in America*. New York: William Morrow and Co., 1986.

_____. *Crime in America*. New York: William Morrow and Co., 1990.

Peck, Robert N. *Arly*. New York: Walker and Co., 1989.

Rossiter, Phyllis. *Moxie*. New York: Four Winds Press, 1990.

Whitmore, Arvella. *The Bread Winner*. Boston: Houghton Mifflin Co., 1990.

Human Rights

Hamanaka, Sheila. *The Journey: Japanese Americans, Racism, and Renewal*. New York: Orchard Books, 1990.

Holbrook, Sabra. *Fighting Back: The Struggle for Gay Rights*. New York: Penguin USA, Lodestar Books, 1987.

Levitin, Sonia. *The Return*. New York: Macmillan Publishing Co., Atheneum Publishers, 1987.

McKissack, Patricia, and Frederick McKissack. *A Long Hard Journey: The Story of Pullman Porter*. New York: Walker and Co., 1989.

Meltzer, Milton. *The Bill of Rights: How We Got It and What It Means*. New York: HarperCollins Publishers, 1990.

Naidoo, Beverly. *Chain of Fire*. New York: HarperCollins Publishers, 1990.

O'Dell, Scott. *My Name Is Not Angelica*. Boston: Houghton Mifflin Co., 1989.

Taylor, Mildred. *The Gold Cadillac*. New York: Penguin USA, Dial Books for Young Readers, 1987.

_____. *Mississippi Bridge*. New York: Penguin USA, Dial Books for Young Readers, 1990.

_____. *The Road to Memphis*. New York: Penguin USA, Dial Books for Young Readers, 1990.

Immigration

Ashabranner, Brent. *Children of the Maya: A Guatemalan Indian Odyssey*. New York: Dodd Mead, 1986.

Ashabranner, Brent, and Melissa Ashabranner. *Into a Strange Land: Unaccompanied Refugee Youth in America*. New York: Dodd Mead, 1987.

Dillon, Eilis. *The Seekers*. New York: Charles Scribner's Sons, 1986.

Hewett, Joan, and Richard R. Hewett. *Hector Lives in the United States Now: The Story of a Mexican-American Child*. New York: HarperCollins Publishers, 1990.

Jacobs, William Jay. *Ellis Island: New Hope in a New Land*. New York: Charles Scribner's Sons, 1990.

Levinson, Riki. *Watch the Stars Come Out*. New York: Penguin USA, Dutton Children's Books, 1985.

Mayerson, Evelyn W. *The Cat Who Escaped from Steerage: A Bubbemeiser*. New York: Charles Scribner's Sons, 1990.

Sewall, Marcia. *The Pilgrims of Plimoth*. New York: Macmillan Publishing Co., Atheneum Publishers, 1986.

Sherman, Eileen B. *Monday in Odessa*. New York: Jewish Publication Society, 1986.

Yee, Paul. *Tales from Gold Mountain: Stories of the Chinese in the New World*. New York: Macmillan Publishing Co., 1990.

War and Peace

Ashabranner, Brent. *Always to Remember: The Story of the Vietnam Veterans Memorial*. New York: Dodd Mead, 1988.

Bunting, Eve. *The Wall*. New York: Clarion Books, 1990.

Durell, Ann, and Marilyn Sach, eds. *The Big Book for Peace*. New York: Penguin USA, Dutton Children's Books, 1990.

Freedman, Russell. *Indian Chiefs*. New York: Holiday House, 1987.

Hauptly, Denis J. *In Vietnam*. New York: Macmillan Publishing Co., Atheneum Publishers, 1985.

Hoobler, Dorothy, and Thomas Hoobler. *Vietnam: Why We Fought—An Illustrated History*. New York: Alfred A. Knopf, 1990.

Lawson, Don. *An Album of the Vietnam War*. New York: Franklin Watts, 1986.

Nelson, Theresa. *And One for All*. New York: Orchard Books, 1989.

Scholes, Katherine. *Peace Begins with You*. Boston: Sierra Club Books, 1990.

Warren, James A. *Portrait of a Tragedy: America and the Vietnam War*. New York: Lothrop, Lee and Shepard Books, 1990.

Chapter Eight

Adopting Exit 109: Literature Promotes Action

Vickie Weiss

The idea of adopting exit 109 grew out of my participation in the 1990 National Geographic Society Summer Institute. Sixty-five educators from various state geographic alliance groups studied together in Washington, D.C., for a month—learning the five themes of geography and sharing lessons and strategies from colleagues and experts in the field.

As part of the NGS Institute, participants developed lessons to use in the classroom. I prepared a lesson that I call "The Riverkeeper and Me" based on *Riverkeeper* by George Ancona (1990), a book listed as a National Council for the Social Studies-

From *Riverkeeper*, © 1990 George Ancona, reprinted by permission of Macmillan Publishing Company.

Children's Book Council Notable Trade Book in the Field of the Social Studies. The concept of a riverkeeper, I thought, would be one that my students could relate to. I knew I would enjoy using this book during the school year. Thus, I decided, I could use *Riverkeeper* to develop the themes of location, place, and human-environment interaction. I enjoyed trying to think of projects and activities related to geographic themes using the book as a point of departure for my students. Little did I know that the best was yet to come.

As the culmination of our study and collaboration, participants in the NGS Institute were treated to a four-day field trip that took us south of Washington, D.C., looping eastward and coming back by way of Chincoteague and the Delmarva Peninsula. When I visited those places for the first time, I marveled at the beauty and necessity of the wetlands. I realized that saving and protecting them was as necessary as preventing the destruction of the rain forests. I pledged to teach my students to care about the wetlands the way the riverkeeper in George Ancona's book cares about the Hudson River.

Adopting a Wetlands Location

When I returned to Grand Blanc, Michigan, I rediscovered the perfect wetland site: exit 109, a loop ramp off a major highway. I had previously been curious about the area because there were thirty to forty lodges on the adjacent pond that I assumed to be either beaver or muskrat homes. Because the wetland site was located down and away from the ramp, it seemed to me that it would lend itself nicely to classroom study and observation. Thus, I decided to adopt the exit ramp as a project for our wetland study.

Out of courtesy (or ignorance), I thought I would be competent and professional and call the Michigan Department of Transportation to inform them of my project. In my mind, they were going to be thrilled and offer me free materials and resource speakers. Instead, the person I first spoke with was furious. He told me that if I entered the site I would be breaking both state and federal regulations and I could be arrested. I was informed that I had no right or permission to take children onto the property. When I asked for a copy of the regulations or how I could apply for permission, the man refused to give me any further information and slammed down the telephone.

At that point, most teachers probably would have given up or at least gone on to Plan B. I just got angry! Once again, I called the Department of Transportation and found two wonderful people, Janet Foran and Carey Rouse, who were willing to help me with the project. First, they tried to find another site that would not be governed by federal highway laws. Carey Rouse met us at a possible site after school one October afternoon. Three student officers of our Kids for Saving the Earth club came along. As we stepped out of our car onto the shoulder, we could feel the wind from cars whizzing by. It was frightening. We all knew at once that although the new site might be less complicated to get permission to use, it was much more dangerous than exit 109. It was also virtually impossible to reach the wetland area from the roadway because of the brush and there were no paths to walk on.

Ms. Rouse went back to her office to check once more with the proper authorities at the Department of Transportation and to ask if we could get a permit to study the wetlands at exit 109. Because it was more protected and safer for the children than the one we had examined, we thought perhaps there was a ray of hope.

Our good news finally came one day in late October. After negotiating, discussing, filling out written permit applications, and talking to both helpful and unhelpful individuals since early August, we received legal permission to visit the site as an educational environmental project.

The students were delighted. We had all driven by the wetlands many times and had kept our fingers crossed. We had lovingly called it "our exit" from the very beginning of the school year and we finally believed it was ours.

Visiting Our Adopted Wetlands

On November 8, 1990, our yellow school bus was escorted onto the shoulder of exit 109 by the Grand Blanc Township Police. Carey Rouse boarded our bus and together we began our long-awaited adventure, feeling a little like explorers of an unknown territory. At last we were to see this land up close with our own eyes.

Walking around the site with Ms. Rouse, the children learned about the area and how it developed. A wildlife biologist, she is familiar with the plants and animals native to the area. The children asked many questions and together they explored the site. As they walked back to the bus at the end of the outing, the students instinctively began to pick up the litter and junk on the property. They loaded it onto the bus to discard back at the school so that their exit would be cleaner. I could see that they had already become like the riverkeeper in Ancona's book.

During the winter months, we developed exit 109 field notebooks. We wrote about our experiences, glued in some reprints of articles about wetlands, and made sketches of animals and plants that lived in the habitat.

The following resources were helpful. "Hanging on to the Wetlands" produced by David Newton and Irwin Slesnick at Western Washington University (1981) contains many teaching activities and information that expanded our knowledge and understanding. *Wading into the Wetlands,* a Ranger Rick Nature Scope sixty-five-page booklet produced by the National Wildlife Federation (1986), was full of background information, craft ideas, resources, and a multitude of projects suitable for all ages studying the wetlands. *Kids for Saving the Earth: Adviser's Club Kit* (1988) was developed by an organization started by 11-year-old Clinton Hill. Now funded by Target, Inc., in his memory, the kit is available free to teachers at Target stores. The colorful materials are well organized, interesting to read, and full of fun projects. The students added these to their collection of earthkeeping things.

On April 12, 1991, we went back to our site with Tim Treadway of the Michigan United Conservation Clubs. The weather was magnificent— blue skies and bright sunshine. Tim brought with him examples of animals that inhabit our type of wetland area. As he brought out each animal the children oohed and aahed. They were thrilled to see a wood duck, a fourteen-pound snapping turtle, a snake, and a mink. As they listened carefully to each word Tim had to say, it seemed the perfect place to learn about the animals— at the wetlands they inhabit.

Reaching the Community

Even the television crew contacted by the MUCC organization had a wonderful time learning about nature that day. A local news reporter who happened to be driving by stopped to see what was happening. The media covered the event of kids studying the wetland area with features both on television and on the front page of the local newspaper. Who knows? Maybe we raised some awareness or concern about the wetlands in the minds of adults that day.

What did I hope would happen as a result of our project? My goal was that the students would always remember a time when they were keepers of the earth. My prediction was that because the area around our exit was such a busy highway, this would not remain a wetland area very long. I believed that the pollution from the exhaust systems would affect both the wetlands and the wildlife. These changes would be a visible sign to my students of just how fragile the earth is and would demonstrate that humans have the capacity both to destroy it and to safeguard it.

As my students drive by exit 109 with their parents they will see the changes that occur. Who knows? Maybe this class will someday meet again at our exit—exit 109—in the year 2000 to see if it is still there. And our whole adventure began with the simple yet powerful message of the NCSS-CBC notable book *Riverkeeper*.

Lesson Plan: The Riverkeeper and Me
Overview

The environment depends on all of us to understand and safeguard it. Students need to be aware of the actions they can take now to participate as concerned citizens of the world. The purpose of this lesson is to begin to involve students in the ownership of a small piece of the world.

Connection to Curriculum

Geography themes: place, location, human-environment interaction; reading and literature; art; science.

Grade Level

4th and 5th grades.

Time

Two forty-minute periods, plus a variety of other times throughout the school year.

Materials

Chart paper.

Resources

Riverkeeper by George Ancona; *Kids for Saving the Earth Guidebook* (one for each student).

Objectives

Students will:
- identify five facts about the Hudson River.
- understand the term *estuary*.
- brainstorm a list of places or things to care for around school, home, or neighborhood.
- analyze ways they can be a keeper of a small part of the world.
- select an area or object to care for.
- create a mini-journal as the keeper of their special site.

Suggested Procedures

1. List items students care for, save, or keep such as baseball cards, stuffed animals, stamps, letters, photographs, or pets. Have students list how they care for or keep these things. What is needed to provide proper care or attention for keeping them in good condition? Write these items on chart paper and hang on the classroom wall.

2. Introduce the book *Riverkeeper* by telling the students that they will hear about an individual that *keeps* something too. Suggest that they listen for the definition, the mission, and the ways that John Cronin cares for the things he keeps. Read the book aloud. At the end of the story, have students recall significant and interesting details.

3. Locate the Hudson River on a classroom map so that children can identify where the story occurs. On a chart or transparency, trace the path of the Hudson River and write some of the details from the story. This will assist in story mapping.

4. Discuss the new word *estuary* which means an arm of the sea at the lower end of a river. Be certain

that students understand that the Atlantic Ocean actually rolls into the Hudson River. This can be demonstrated as a science experiment with warm water meeting cool water. Ask students to pretend that the Atlantic Ocean is meeting the Hudson River. This can be shown in a clear plastic tub on the overhead projector.

5. Write the definition of *riverkeeper* on the chalkboard or a transparency. List environmental places that the children could care for around their school, home, or neighborhood. Add these suggested places to another chart and post it in the room. You might develop catchy descriptions such as "sidewalk saver," "trail trooper," or "pond protector."

6. Visit the places mentioned around the school or neighborhood. If possible, have students clean up the areas mentioned or beautify them in some way. (For example, a city school could remove litter and add small barrel flower gardens.)

7. Students select a site to be the keeper of for a specific duration of time—a week, a month, or a semester. They can work individually, in pairs, or in small groups. Allow time for students to care for their adopted property. If students do this off school property, periodically have them visit their sites and write in a mini-journal about the experience.

Evaluation

- Can students see ways they can improve the environment?
- Can students write five facts about *Riverkeeper*?
- Can students write a comparison between their effort and what John Cronin did?
- Can students locate the Hudson River and define *estuary*?

Extending the Lesson

- Have the class write a letter to John Cronin, the riverkeeper.
- Create a mini-journal of what students accomplish each time they care for their site.
- Record in sketches, photographs, or video the activity and changes in the area.
- Develop a sign or way to identify the caretaker of the area (like an adopt-a-highway sign).
- Visit a nature center or preserve to talk to caretakers.
- Analyze improvements in the sites through graphing techniques.
- Raise money to purchase or build items to beautify or maintain area.

Connections

This introduction would lead naturally to the "Kids for Saving the Earth" program. The program was started by Clinton Hill, an 11-year-old boy from Minnesota who wondered what he could do about pollution. He got other kids from his 6th grade class interested and they formed a club. Clinton Hill died of cancer, but his family and friends have carried on his interests. Target, Inc., learned about the story and now funds the program offering many wonderful materials for students and teachers.

References

Ancona, George. *Riverkeeper*. New York: Macmillan Publishing Co., 1990.

Kids for Saving the Earth: Adviser's Club Kit. 1988. Available free from Target department stores to teachers and others who work with groups of children.

Newton, David, and Irwin Slesnick. "Hanging on to the Wetlands." Book I. Bellingham: Western Washington University, 1981.

"Wading into Wetlands." Washington, D.C.: National Wildlife Federation, 1986.

Chapter Nine
Books in Brief Bolster Learning

Jane Brem

I use children's books whether I teach primary, intermediate, middle, or graduate school. Using the books is a great way to develop a concept, model a project, or initiate interest in a topic. The following descriptions provide examples of how you can easily incorporate children's trade books into your instruction. For a more complete explanation of the strategies exemplified here, see "Concept Learning: Three Strategies," in *Social Studies in Elementary Education* (Jarolimek and Parker 1993).

Concept Formation

Example One

A 4th grade class, as part of a unit titled "People and Their Government," is studying the judicial system. The teacher, Ms. Matsuyama, orchestrates a lesson about fairness in the following way.

After getting the students comfortably organized in the reading corner of the classroom, Ms. Matsuyama shows students the book *Strega Nona*, an old tale retold by Tomie dePaola (1975). She tells the students that the story is about a person named Big Anthony who creates a problem for himself. She then directs the students to listen carefully so they can identify how the problem was created and how it was resolved. After students respond, Ms. Matsuyama reads the selection again. This time she tells the students they may want to pay close attention to how other people react to Big Anthony and his problem.

Ms. Matsuyama then has the students return to their desks and she distributes a data retrieval chart shown in figure 1. She demonstrates how to complete the chart by facilitating a discussion about the three focus questions and how they relate to Big Anthony. She has the students work in small groups to discuss the same three questions in relation to the three enumerated situations. Because Ms. Matsuyama realizes that her 4th graders may need help with details associated with such situations, she monitors the groups closely and asks prompting questions such as the following: Was it made clear that all work had to be completed beforehand? Why were different play areas identified? She also encourages the students to discuss the situation with their parents or guardians, assigning completion of the chart as homework.

The next day, after verifying that all the necessary information has been recorded, Ms. Matsuyama asks how these four situations are different and how they are similar. She records their responses to the second question on the chalkboard and then instructs the students to take a few minutes to write down a summary of these similarities in one sentence beginning with "People are treated…" After the students compose their definitions, the teacher takes time to allow sharing and provides the students feedback. The students then compose a second draft, taking more care to include the data generated by their focus questions.

Ms. Matsuyama asks the students to think of or invent a word that describes these situations. After several examples have been shared, the teacher tells the students that the conventional label or name for these circumstances is "fairness." Then, to have the students reinforce, extend, and refine their conception of fairness, Ms. Matsuyama involves the students in one or more of the following application activities.

1. She shows posters of situations in which the viewer can infer if someone is being treated fairly or unfairly. She asks the students to distinguish examples and nonexamples of fairness and requests that the students present reasons for their decisions.

2. She has small groups of students write a story in which the main character is treated in a fair or unfair manner. She reminds the students to include the rules associated with the situation. She also encourages students to create characters with various opinions.

3. She describes several situations in which a person is treated unfairly and asks how the situation might be changed so that fairness is present.

Figure 1. Focus Questions

	Should everyone have to follow the same rules?	How do people's opinions influence their decisions?	Is anyone identified as "the favorite" or is everyone treated the same?
Big Anthony			
When a student isn't allowed to go on a class field trip because of incomplete assignments…			
When girls and boys have different dress codes (e.g., boys can wear shorts and girls can't)…			
When the playground policy doesn't allow a star 1st grade baseball player to join the 5th grade team because there are separate areas for primary and intermediate grades			

Example Two

While studying "Our Community" with his second graders, Mr. Sanchez introduces a lesson to develop the historical concept of "change" by offering his students the data retrieval chart shown in figure 2. He then tells his students that as he reads the book *The Little House* by Virginia L. Burton (1942), he wants them to write down the differences they hear and see in the buildings, transportation, and people's behavior.

After reading and talking about the noted differences, Mr. Sanchez directs the students to add the following to boxes A, B, and C in the left-hand column of their chart:

Box A: My neighborhood
Box B: Where my mother, father, or guardian grew up
Box C: Where a grandparent or old friend grew up

Mr. Sanchez then proceeds with the following steps in a similar manner as exemplified in the example with Ms. Matsuyama:

Step 1: Study multiple examples.
Step 2: Note differences.
Step 3: Note similarities.
Step 4: Summarize similarities in a sentence.
Step 5: Label or name.
Step 6: Classify with applications by distinguishing examples and nonexamples, creating a new example or correcting nonexamples.

How Perceptions Influence Classification: List, Group, Label

To introduce the study of a nation, a teacher might follow the example demonstrated by Ms. Eaglestaff when she opened one of her 7th grade classes by asking, "When I say 'China,' what comes to mind?" Ms. Eaglestaff writes their responses on the chalkboard. The beginning of the list might look like this:

• rice paddies
• the Great Wall
• crowded cities
• chopsticks
• Mao

After the chalkboard is filled with ideas, she asks each student to take a piece of scrap paper, group together things that seem to fit together, and offer a reason why they make a group. During this process she will point out how the same thing can fit in various categories because people perceive the same things in different ways.

When the group has exhausted the category process, Ms. Eaglestaff shows the students *A Kid's Catalog of Israel* by Chaya M. Burstein (1988), a compilation of interesting facts, people, stories, and songs associated with Israel. She tells the students how this book may serve as a reference for the students' class project—the creation of a book entitled *A Kid's Catalog of China*. Accordingly, Ms. Eaglestaff has created interest in a long-term project. While her students outline, research, write, edit, and produce a book, they will refer to the book on Israel as a model.

Introducing an Aspect of Culture

Children's trade books can provide an effective avenue to introduce an aspect of culture. Note the ways the following three teachers used a trade book.

• As a way of introducing Japanese vocabulary to her 6th graders, Ms. Sharkey reads *Momotaro: The Peach Boy*, a traditional Japanese tale retold by Linda Shute (1986). She points out how the illustrations

In Two Worlds: *A Yup'ik Eskimo Family*

Aylette Jenness and Alice Rivers   Photographs by Aylette Jenness

From *In Two Worlds: A Yup'ik Eskimo Family* © 1989 Aylette Jenness and Alice Rivers, reprinted by permission of Houghton Mifflin Company.

Figure 2. Focus Questions

	How are buildings different?	How is transportation different?	How do people act differently?
The Little House			
A			
B			
C			

depict the spectacle of medieval Japanese painted scrolls.

- Commencing a study of African geography and how animals adapt to their respective environments, 3d grade teacher Mr. Hasse reads *Why Mosquitoes Buzz in People's Ears* by Verna Aardena (1975). This book not only identifies what animals the students will investigate, but it shows how similar this folktale is to the story "This Is the House that Jack Built."

- Showing photographs from *In Two Worlds: A Yup'ik Eskimo Family* by Aylette Jenness and Alice Rivers (1989), Ms. Banks points out to her urban 1st graders how a family living in a small Alaskan town adopts modern ways without losing old traditions. This provides an example for these urban children to compare and contrast their daily habits with those of the family in Alaska.

Conclusion

The examples illuminated in this chapter demonstrate ways to use children's trade books when teaching students of all ages. Similar examples and strategies have been demonstrated with high school students and with practitioners who are students in graduate curriculum and instruction courses. It is important to recognize how a reading selection—whether a children's book, a periodical article, or an adult book—can be used with similar strategies. Thus, books in brief can bolster learning!

References

Aardena, Verna. *Why Mosquitoes Buzz in People's Ears*. New York: Penguin USA, Dial Books for Young Readers, 1975.

Burstein, Chaya M. *A Kid's Catalog of Israel*. Philadelphia: Jewish Publication Society, 1988.

Burton, Virginia L. *The Little House*. Boston: Houghton Mifflin Co., 1942.

dePaola, Tomie. *Strega Nona*. Englewood Cliffs, N.J.: Prentice-Hall, 1975.

Jarolimek, John, and Walter Parker. *Social Studies in Elementary Education*. 9th ed. New York: Macmillan Publishing Co., 1993.

Jenness, Aylette, and Alice Rivers. *In Two Worlds: A Yup'ik Eskimo Family*. Boston: Houghton Mifflin Co., 1989.

Shute, Linda. *Momotaro: The Peach Boy*. New York: Lothrop, Lee and Shepard Books, 1986.

Chapter Ten

Developing Literature Packets to Foster Social Studies Learning

Judith S. Wooster

I am hard pressed to find a children's book that doesn't have social studies potential. Children's books are about people, problems, places, and perspectives—all of which are the stuff of social studies. Yet putting books in students' hands is not sufficient if our goal is to provide meaningful social studies learning. However rich these literature resources, we must plan purposefully to capitalize on the potential of children's books for teaching social studies. Many teachers are doing so.

Social Studies in the Morning?

It is prime time on Tuesday morning, and students in this busy 2d grade are working on social studies. Although social studies is often relegated to the available afternoon hours in the tightly packed elementary school day, this classroom is different. The skillful teacher has integrated several parts of the curriculum around an interdisciplinary theme from his local social studies curriculum guide. The theme is a common one at the elementary level: "Families Here and There, Then and Now."

On this particular morning, four students are meeting with their teacher at a small table. Each student has one of a series of four books by cultural anthropologist Ole Hertz about Tobias, a young boy growing up in Greenland. As the students flip through the books, the teacher asks them to focus on things the pictures show about Tobias and his family. Peter notes that they don't live in an igloo like he thought they would. Maria shows a picture in her book that indicates they sometimes do. She volunteers to read to find out more. They have birthdays and cakes too, contributes Joseph in a soft voice. The fourth child in the group seems more curious about the globe on the table; she spins it once, drawing the attention of the group by putting a lump of clay and a flag on

Greenland where Tobias lives. Before they leave the group, their teacher reviews how to use the information retrieval chart in their manila folder packets. The chart is a grid upon which students record information from their books about the homes, food, fun, land, and customs of families in their books. The teacher reminds students to make notes in words or pictures as they read about Tobias's family. They will use these picture notes to make a chart for the class.

At another table, wearing headphones and looking at another set of books, three students are learning about the life of Jafta, a young South African boy, from a series of books by Hugh Lewin. One of the three students is beginning to draw pictures on her blank information retrieval chart. Another is logging the title of the book he is reading. He puts his log into a folder and files the folder in a milk crate on the side counter.

An author study table set up in the reading corner focuses this month on Tomie dePaola. The teacher chose this author because many of his books focus on families and discuss key ideas the teacher wants to convey to his social studies students. He wants students to become interested and skilled in asking and answering social science questions. To help in this task, he has taken great care to select a group of books focused on these understandings. A study packet he developed helps his students focus on important content, concepts, and skills. Although students in this class sometimes use textbooks for reference and small-group instruction, they depend most heavily on children's trade books to help them build social studies understandings.

Deciding on a Curricular Theme

Talking with the 2d grade teacher, we learn that he began his planning by identifying a theme from the local curriculum that would lend itself well to a trade book approach. He generally plans his themes or units a year at a time, in the fall, so that he can adapt his program to the needs of his new students and collect as many books as possible for upcoming units.

Mapping or Webbing the Key Ideas for the Theme or Unit

This 2d grade teacher uses a theme web or map to identify the key ideas that become the core of his units. Identifying the key social science ideas is perhaps the most challenging part of the planning process. Content should be significant, accurate, and concise. Ideas come from looking at the local curriculum guide, browsing through a variety of textbooks, and talking with other teachers. This teacher wants students to know and understand that families are found in all societies, past and present. And that although family structures may differ in type, they serve as the basic unit for passing on customs, traditions, and values to the young, and provide basic human needs of food, shelter, and clothing. They also provide love and a sense of belonging.

The teacher wants students to understand that families are interdependent. At the same time, he wants to root these important understandings in content, by studying families in specific times and places in order to develop this awareness in his students. His web or map (figure 1) identifies these social science ideas for the theme "Families Here and There, Then and Now."

Selecting Books to Develop the Key Ideas

With the main ideas of the unit in mind, the teacher selected books guided by book lists such as the annual National Council for the Social Studies-Children's Book Council Notable Children's Trade Books in the Field of Social Studies list, and lists found in the *School Library Journal* and *The Horn Book* magazine. He also consulted with his library media specialist and the reading teacher next door who runs a literature-based reading program. Among the outstanding books identified for this unit were Ann Grifalconi's *Village of Round and Square Houses* (1986), Marcia Sewall's *People of the Breaking Day* (1990), *The Chalk Doll* by Charlotte Pomerantz

From *The Chalk Doll*, © 1989 illustrations by Frané Lessac, reprinted by permission of HarperCollins Publishers.

(1989), *In Coal Country* by Judith Hendershot (1987), *My Sister's Wedding* by Richard Rosenblum (1987), *Family Farm* by Thomas Locker (1988), and *Least of All* by Carol Purdy (1990).

As he began to identify relevant books, the teacher noted that many books by Barbara Cooney such as *Island Boy* (1988), *Miss Rumphius* (1982), and *Ox-Cart Man* (1979) were well suited to the theme. Likewise, many Tomie dePaola books such as *Nana Upstairs, Nana Downstairs* (1973) and *Now One Foot, Now the Other* (1981) focus on key ideas in the theme. Therefore, he decided to study these two exceptional authors. He also included in the collection several photo essays such as *In Two Worlds: A Yup'ik Eskimo Family* by Aylette Jenness and Alice Rivers (1989) and *The American Family Farm* by Joan Anderson (1989) with photographs by George Ancona to introduce his students to that genre.

Developing an Activity Packet to Guide Students as They Read

The next step in the planning process is to devel-

Figure 1. Theme Web for Families Here and There, Then and Now

A theme web centered on "Families Here and There, Then and Now" with connected branches:

- **Families teach the young**: customs and traditions, language, cultural heritage, values
- **Families vary in structure**
- **Families change over time**
- **Families provide for basic needs**: food, shelter, clothing, love
- **Family members are independent**
- **Families are found in all societies**: past, present, U.S., global

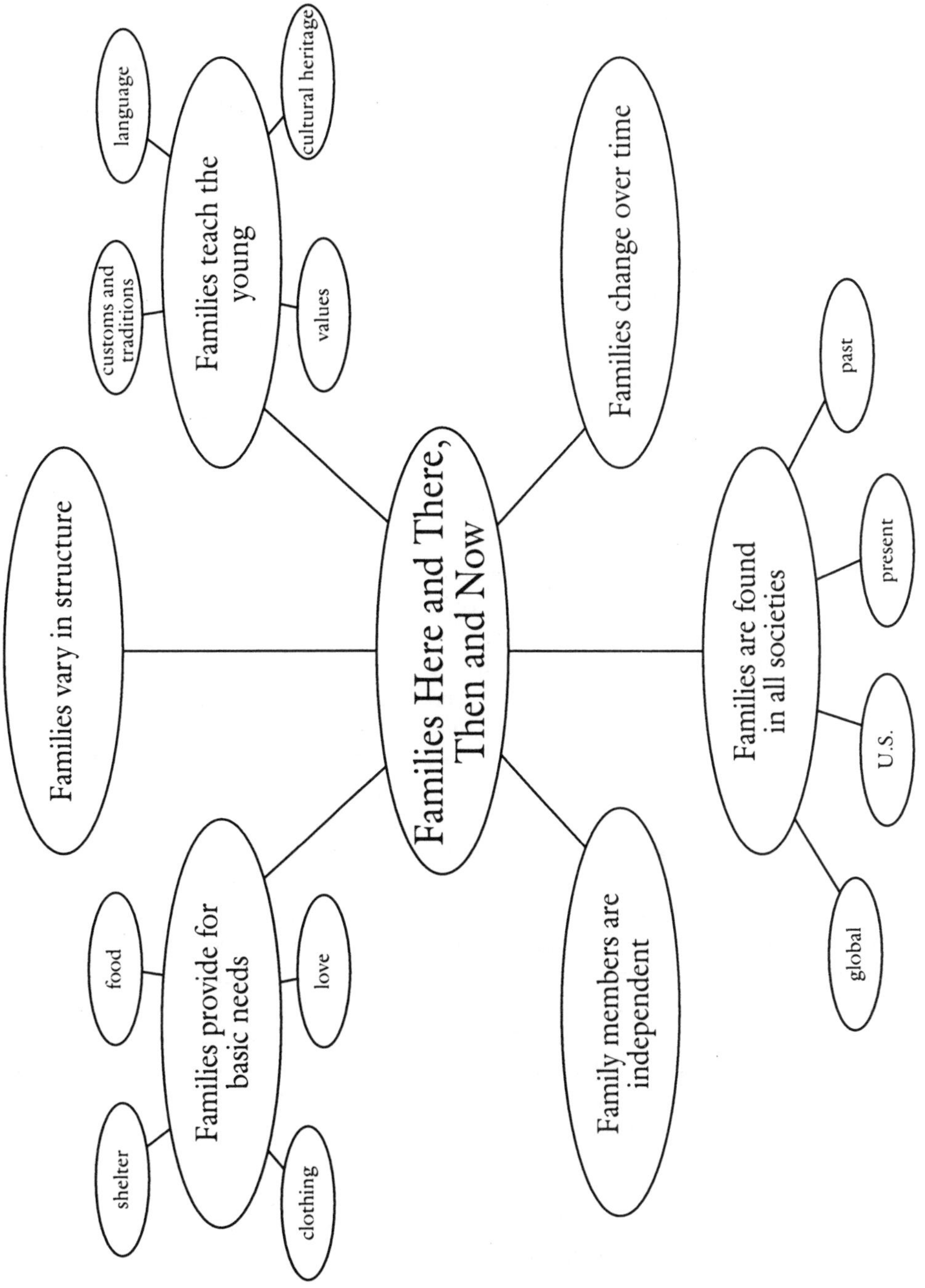

op a packet of activities that will guide students to develop targeted social science understandings as they read. A packet of activities can both help students focus on content and concepts and develop skills. Packet activities also offer potential as evaluative tools. They are both instructional devices and windows into students' understanding. Each activity is purposefully planned to develop students' social science understanding.

For the "Families Here and There, Then and Now" theme, the teacher developed a packet that included a family tree on which students charted their own family or any family from their reading. The teacher planned to use the completed trees in small-group and whole-class discussions to help students understand that family structures vary, and that family members are interdependent.

The teacher also included in the activity packet an information retrieval chart on which students would take notes in words and pictures. The chart was designed to help students focus on how the families in their stories met their basic needs. These charts would also become sources of information for mapping where families in the books live, placing the families on a time line, and comparing and contrasting families across time and space.

The students used a Venn diagram of overlapping circles as a device to assist them in comparing their own family to a trade book family or in comparing two trade book families. The area of overlap in the diagram represents characteristics shared by the two families, while the remainder of each circle shows the unique characteristics of each family (figure 2).

The 2d graders in this classroom keep their activity packets in manila folders. Completed work is frequently posted because it serves as information from which others may learn. The class creates gallery showings, bulletin boards, and hall displays to share information with others. Charts, graphs, and diagrams are often a part of such displays. Parents can see this social studies and language program in action and frequently comment on the level of enthusiasm their children feel for their work.

Figure 2. Information Referral Chart

Name: _____ Book: _____
Family Members: _____

Home	
Food	
Fun	
Customs	

Venn Diagram

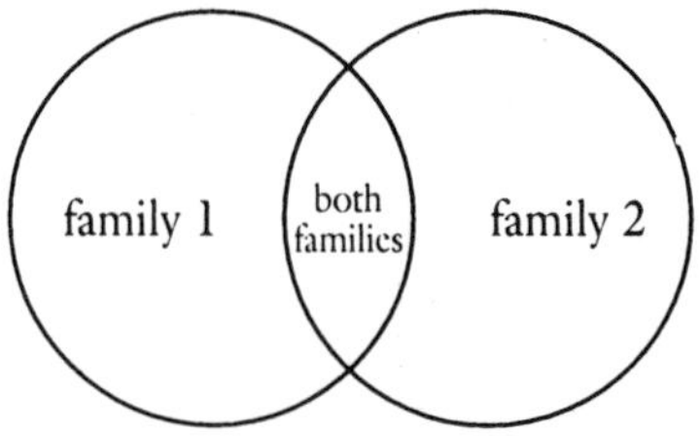

family 1   both families   family 2

Applying the Approach to Other Levels and Topics

Although the theme "Families Here and There, Then and Now" is a 2d grade example, the planning process for creating theme units and activity packets is similar at any level. The process involves

- developing a year's plan of curricular themes;
- mapping or webbing the key ideas for the theme or unit;
- selecting books to develop the key ideas; and
- developing an activity packet to guide students as they read.

The following examples illustrate the same approach applied to a 4th grade unit on immigration.

An Immigration Insights Theme Packet
Developing a Year's Plan of Curricular Themes

This grade 4 unit on immigration was designed as part of a year-long study of key periods in U.S. history.

Figure 3. Theme Web for "Immigration Insights"

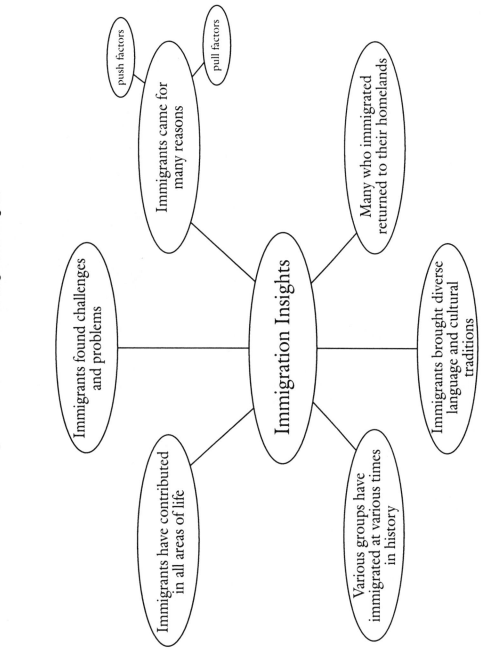

Among the other in-depth themes to be taught this year are "Sea to Shining Sea," a unit focusing on geography and ecology, and "The First Americans, Yesterday and Today," which focuses on Native Americans from historical and contemporary perspectives. The unit on "Immigration Insights" was selected because of the range of materials available on the topic suitable to the reading levels of middle grade readers. The unit also stresses important multicultural topics of diversity and pluralism through compelling, high-interest stories.

Mapping or Webbing the Key Ideas for the Theme or Unit

The key ideas of the "Immigration Insights" theme are shown on the web in figure 3. These ideas provide the focus for the theme's activities. Desired student outcomes grow from the web, as do evaluation approaches and strategies.

Selecting Books to Develop the Key Ideas

The rich variety of literature on this topic made the task of identifying books relatively easy. Among the many titles selected for the study were Betty Bao Lord's *In the Year of the Boar and Jackie Robinson* (1984), Brent and Melissa Ashabranner's *Into a Strange Land: Unaccompanied Refugee Youth in America* (1987), *New Americans* by Ashabranner and Paul Conklin (1983), Riki Levinson's *Watch the Stars Come Out* (1985), Leonard Everett Fisher's *Ellis Island: Gateway to the World* (1986), Alice Fleming's *The King of Prussia and a Peanut Butter Sandwich* (1988), Alan Lelchuck's *On Home Ground* (1987), Katherine Paterson's *Park's Quest* (1988), Evelyn Wilde Mayerson's *The Cat Who Escaped from Steerage* (1990), William Jay Jacob's *Ellis Island: New Hope in a New Land* (1990), Joan and Richard Hewett's *Hector Lives in the United States Now: The Story of a Mexican-American Child* (1990), Paul Yee's *Tales from Gold Mountain: Stories of the Chinese in the New World* (1990), and *Lion Dancer: Ernie Wan's Chinese New Year* by Kate Waters and Madeline Slovenz-Low (1990). A study of Ann Pellowski, Lawrence Yen, and Yoshiko Uchida's works complemented this theme. Because

EVELYN WILDE MAYERSON

The Cat Who Escaped from Steerage

From *The Cat Who Escaped from Steerage*, © 1990 Evelyn Wilde Mayerson, reprinted by permission of Macmillan Publishing Company.

these authors' books address key ideas, they merited in-depth study.

Identifying books with a range of reading levels allows students appropriate challenge without frustration, as they select books to develop theme-based understandings. Selecting fiction and nonfiction sources representing a variety of genres expands students' literary awareness and enriches the language arts program.

Developing an Activity Packet to Guide Students as They Read

This grade 4 teacher was especially interested in providing purposeful activities to develop the theme. At the same time, she wanted to foster the joy of reading and was eager to avoid burdensome and tedious written activities. She developed an activity

Figure 4. Sample Activity Packet

Immigration Insights through Literature

Both fiction and nonfiction books can help you learn more about the people who have come to the United States. As you read your book, record details to help you share your ideas with others.

Your name _____ Date begun: _____ ended: _____

Book title: _____ Author: _____

Publisher: _____ Date of publication: _____

1. **Select Snippets:** As you read your book, think about sections you'd like to read to others. You might choose sections of a few pages or even an entire chapter. Try to select parts that would help your listener understand more about immigration, an immigrant group, or a single immigrant.

Section	Pages	Reason Selected

2. **Some Basic Questions:**

Who immigrated? _____

When? _____

Figure 4. Continued

Where did they arrive? _____

Where did they settle? _____

Why did they come? _____

3. **Describe Living Conditions of the Immigrants:** _____

_____

_____

_____

4. **Use the Chart Below** (and other paper if necessary), to record any problems the immigrants encountered.

Problem Encountered	How Handled	Pages noted

5. **In Your Journal,** keep a list of questions you have as you read your book. We will use these questions to guide our study of immigrant groups.
6. **In Your Journal,** keep a list of interesting ideas you learned while reading this book.

packet that related to all the books her students were reading. The packet guided students to consider social science ideas as they read, while avoiding ponderous record keeping and writing. The packet is reproduced in figure 4.

As students read their books and completed their packets, they shared their growing body of information in small groups. They made generalizations and synthesized ideas about immigration in the United States. Student-generated questions guided further reading and research using a wide range of sources including textbooks, almanacs, telephone books, atlases, diaries, and journals. Students shared books and read passages to one another. A reader's theater program that grew from these activities was presented to parents and other students. Oral interviews and visitors to the classroom provided additional insights into immigration. Students emerged with a rich understanding of immigration in the United States and a deep interest in continuing their learning about the topic.

As seen in these glimpses of a grade 2 and grade 4 classroom, trade books are excellent sources for developing social science content, concepts, and skills. The teacher must, however, plan purposefully to capture the power of these resources in the elementary classroom. Planning involves focusing on key social science ideas, selecting appropriate literature sources, and developing activities to foster student understanding of targeted social science content, concepts, and skills. The benefits include enhanced student interest and learning as well as effective use of valuable classroom instructional time.

References

Anderson, Joan. *The American Family Farm*. San Diego: Harcourt Brace Jovanovich, 1989.

Ashabranner, Brent, and Melissa Ashabranner. *Into a Strange Land: Unaccompanied Refugee Youth in America*. New York: Dodd, 1987.

Ashabranner, Brent, and Paul Conklin. *New Americans*. New York: G. P. Putnam's Sons, 1983.

Cooney, Barbara. *Ox-Cart Man*. New York: Penguin USA, Viking, 1979.

_____. *Miss Rumphius*. New York: Penguin USA, Viking, 1982.

_____. *Island Boy*. New York: Penguin USA, Viking, 1988.

dePaola, Tomie. *Nana Upstairs, Nana Downstairs*. New York: G. P. Putnam's Sons, 1973.

_____. *Strega Nona*. New Jersey: Prentice-Hall, 1975.

_____. *Now One Foot, Now the Other*. New York: G. P. Putnam's Sons, 1981.

Fisher, Leonard Everett. *Ellis Island: Gateway to the World*. New York: Holiday House, 1986.

Fleming, Alice. *The King of Prussia and a Peanut Butter Sandwich*. New York: Macmillan Publishing Co., 1988.

Grifalconi, Ann. *Village of Round and Square Houses*. Boston: Little, Brown and Co., 1986.

Hendershot, Judith. *In Coal Country*. New York: Alfred A. Knopf, 1987.

Hertz, Ole. *Tobias Catches Trout*. Minneapolis, Minn.: Carolrhoda Books, 1984.

_____. *Tobias Goes Ice Fishing*. Minneapolis, Minn.: Carolrhoda Books, 1984.

_____. *Tobias Goes Seal Hunting*. Minneapolis, Minn.: Carolrhoda Books, 1984.

_____. *Tobias Has a Birthday*. Minneapolis, Minn.: Carolrhoda Books, 1984.

Hewett, Joan, and Richard R. Hewett. *Hector Lives in the United States Now: The Story of a Mexican-American Child*. New York: HarperCollins Publishers, 1990.

Jacob, William Jay. *Ellis Island: New Hope in a New Land*. New York: Macmillan Publishing Co., 1990.

Jenness, Aylette, and Alice Rivers. *In Two Worlds: A Yup'ik Eskimo Family*. Boston: Houghton Mifflin Co., 1989.

Lelchuck, Alan. *On Home Ground*. New York: Harcourt Brace Jovanovich, 1987.

Levinson, Riki. *Watch the Stars Come Out*. New York: Penguin USA, Dutton Children's Books, 1985.

Lewin, Hugh. *Jafta and the Wedding*. Minneapolis, Minn.: Carolrhoda Books, 1983.

_____. *Jafta's Father*. Minneapolis, Minn.: Carolrhoda Books, 1983.

_____. *Jafta's Mother*. Minneapolis, Minn.: Carolrhoda Books, 1983.

_____. *Jafta: The Journey*. Minneapolis, Minn.: Carolrhoda Books, 1984.

_____. *Jafta: The Town*. Minneapolis, Minn.: Carolrhoda Books, 1984.

_____. *Jafta*. Minneapolis, Minn.: Carolrhoda Books, 1989.

Locker, Thomas. *Family Farm*. New York: Penguin USA, Dial Books for Young Readers, 1988.

Lord, Betty Bao. *In the Year of the Boar and Jackie Robinson*. New York: HarperCollins Publishers, 1984.

Mayerson, Evelyn Wilde. *The Cat Who Escaped from Steerage*. New York: Macmillan Publishing Co., 1990.

Paterson, Katherine. *Park's Quest*. New York: HarperCollins Publishers, 1988.

Pomerantz, Charlotte. *The Chalk Doll*. New York: HarperCollins Publishers, 1989.

Purdy, Carol. *Least of All*. New York: Macmillan Publishing Co., 1990.

Rosenblum, Richard. *My Sister's Wedding*. New York: William Morrow and Company, 1987.

Sewall, Marcia. *People of the Breaking Day*. New York: Atheneum Publishers, 1990.

Waters, Kate, and Madeline Slovenz-Low. *Lion Dancer: Ernie Wan's Chinese New Year*. New York: Scholastic, 1990.

Yee, Paul. *Tales from Gold Mountain: Stories of the Chinese in the New World*. New York: Macmillan Publishing Co., 1990.

Chapter Eleven

Using Literature Folders

Alvis T. Harthern

Although the content of social studies can be suspenseful, intriguing, dramatic, and often contradictory, many students do not find it interesting (Savage and Armstrong 1992; VanSickle 1990). Children's literature can recapture excitement for children who have become bored by the textbook accounts of the past (Levstik 1989). Literature can offer children authentic glimpses of daily life in a past era. Young learners can vicariously experience other times, other places, and other life-styles as they think backward in time. Through stories, "they can learn about the people, values, beliefs, hardships, and physical surroundings that were common for a particular time period" (Norton 1992, 382). As children develop a deep understanding of the lives of others, they can improve their understanding of themselves and their heritage. They will understand that today's life is affected by what people did in the past.

Choosing Authentic Literature

One enduring aspect of literature is that it tells a story. The use of authentic historic literature "enables history to become a story well told" (Zarrillo 1989, 18). Through these stories, children feel as though they are in the story setting because they can identify with its characters and events.

Social studies teachers cannot assume that just any literature book will substitute for a textbook. They must carefully choose the trade books they will use. When selecting historical fiction, teachers must look for books that have authentic settings, develop realistic characters, and reflect the experiences, conflicts, and problem resolutions of the time.

They must also carefully plan the activities children will participate in while reading these books. It is not uncommon for pupils to lose interest in an outstanding piece of literature because of the activities assigned by the teacher to guide them through their reading (Norton 1992).

Because of the many layers in good stories, students who read them over and over can gain something new from each reading. This process is called multipass reading (Savage and Armstrong 1992). Each time children return to an event, a time, or a set of characters during the rereading of a book, they will improve their understanding of the story and the social studies content. Not only will they want to reread an exciting piece of literature, they will often read other related literature because they will want to know more about an aspect of the topic (Levstik 1990).

Identifying Strands in Literature Folders

A teacher can organize literature in the social studies classroom in many ways. One way is through the use of literature folders. Folders can be designed depending on the classroom teacher's intended purpose; each folder, however, should contain at least three strands of activities. All three strands should guide the development of social studies knowledge and skills—they just approach it differently. For this paper, I chose three strands. One strand leads students to study the book with its illustrations so that they can gain social studies knowledge. The second focuses on the students' use of skills to gain data and report it (which will also enhance students' proficiency in many skills that come both from the social studies or from other parts of the curriculum). The third strand encourages students' creative expression as they demonstrate their understanding of the social studies content. The questions included should ask students to do more than simply recall facts and should engage students in their construction of knowledge.

Teachers may develop a variety of additional strands, depending on the book selected and the reasons for using the book. If the book has a special vocabulary, for example, one strand could be established around the vocabulary. If the chosen book is strong in economic content, a strand could focus on this. The teacher must examine each book individually to determine which strands to include.

Introducing the Core Book

The book *Ox-Cart Man* (Hall 1979) can serve as a core book to illustrate the use of folders to study life in early nineteenth-century New England. Teachers can use this book in the social studies program at many grade levels.

To introduce the book to the students, display a copy of *Ox-Cart Man*. Have students make predictions about the story by discussing what they see in the illustrations on the front and back covers of the book. Ask where and when they believe the story takes place. Ask students to predict the plot after careful analysis of the back cover. Record their predictions on a chart for future use. Predicting is important because it "helps to set a purpose for reading, keeps children focused on the story, and seems to aid overall comprehension" (Routman 1988, 39).

Instruct students to listen to the story to determine if their predictions were accurate. Then read the story without comments or questions until you come to the place in the story where the ox-cart man goes into the Portsmouth Market. Show the book illustration of the inside of the market. Divide students into groups of three or four and have them predict what they think the father will purchase at the market. As each group shares its predictions (and the basis of its predictions), record them on the predictions chart. Then finish the story and focus on all of the predictions. Discuss the accuracy of the predictions. Help students to understand that even though some predictions were not accurate, they may have been logical.

Explain that the author wrote this story in what is called "circle form." On a large sheet of paper, start drawing the first events in the story. Continue the story and have students suggest items that should go in the circle as they appear in the story. To increase understanding of the circular aspects of a story, discuss other stories written in this form, such as *Charlie Needs a Cloak* (dePaola 1973) and *Rosie's Walk* (Hutchins 1968).

Using Literature Folders

After students complete these activities, divide them into cooperative learning groups for further study of the social studies content in *Ox-Cart Man*. Give each group a work folder and several copies of *Ox-Cart Man*. Each folder should contain questions and activities from the three described strands to guide the group's study of nineteenth-century New England.

Students study the questions and tasks in the folder assigned to the group to make sure they understand them. The students then plan how to accomplish the assignments in their folder. They must decide how the group will accomplish each task. Is there a task that can best be accomplished by a single member of the group? Who is that member? Which task will require more than one student to work together? Who will work together? Is there one activity that requires the entire group to complete it? Is there an order in which the activities will need to be completed?

Encourage students to raise questions about aspects of the story that they would like to understand better or know more about. Discuss these questions with the rest of the class. If the questions are not already in another group's folder they may be added or substituted for one of the teacher's original assignments. Encourage students to continue raising new questions throughout the study. As new questions arise, write them on a "want-to-know" chart. Throughout the study, have students share with each other as they find information about any item on the want-to-know chart.

Because the research process is an important part of the folder concept, students plan their research together. McGinley and Madigan's (1990) "I-Search" strategy offers excellent suggestions for helping students develop their research skills. Before beginning the research, students discuss where they might find information about their assigned tasks. Once they start their data collection, they keep a record of the sources examined and describe how each was helpful. Have them record the useful information they find from each source. The sources should be varied—printed materials, people, field experiences, and audiovisual media. Students continue advising one another, recommending possible new sources of information. At the end of the study, all students explain their research process and the sources they found helpful. This will aid classmates as they begin similar research projects in the future.

Each group also decides how to share their research findings and activities with the entire class. For example, a group in one classroom decided they would build a small ox-cart from a box and put their data inside the cart. Another decided to hold their research in a large sack like those that held the wool. A third group summarized their work in big book form.

Preparing Literature Folders

Consider the physical makeup of the folder. For this study, the teacher might make the folders in the shape of an ox-cart. The illustration on the front side of the folder should relate to the core book. The other three sides should contain questions and activ-

ities from each of the three strands. The model folder can be made from a sturdy file folder that will last, especially if it is laminated. Pockets attached to the folder can hold small task cards.

Pay careful attention to the questions and activities. Questions should be both content-specific and open-ended. The sample questions below are not classified by strand because the strand assignment will depend on background knowledge and experiences of the students.

Sample Content Questions

- What are shingles? What do you think people would do with shingles?
- Why did people want goose feathers?
- What is a honeycomb?
- What kind of food did the ox-cart man take with him to sell?
- What is a barlow knife?

Figure 1

OX-CART MAN

Study the book and its illustrations carefully to complete these activities.

by Donald Hall

1. Make a chart of family members' chores. Indicate which chores were accomplished by single members and which by the entire family working together. Put an "**x**" by the chore you think is the best one to do; put an "**xx**" by the chore you think is most difficult to do.

Chore	Done by whom
Shear sheep	All the family
Knit mittens	The girl

2. Some of the chores may be new to you. Learn about each so you can explain to someone else.

    a. Making shingles -- What are shingles? What are they used for?

    b. Gathering goose feathers -- Why do people need these?

Do people do either of these chores today?

1. Find out through research how many miles per day a person could walk with an ox pulling a loaded cart.

2. Locate Portsmouth, New Hampshire, on a map.

3. Decide where the ox-cart man's farm could be located. Defend your location.

4. Draw a pictorial map illustrating the route the ox-cart man took from his farm to Portsmouth. (Read carefully what your book tells you.)

5. This summer, plan to take the same trip the ox-cart man took. Look at a modern-day map. What towns and cities would you visit?

6. Find the current price of the item the ox-cart man purchased. How much would it cost him if he lived today? How much would he pay in coins?

Sales Slip
Kettle
Needle
Candy
$_____

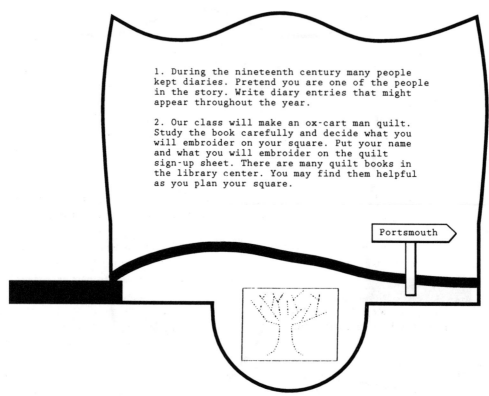

1. During the nineteenth century many people kept diaries. Pretend you are one of the people in the story. Write diary entries that might appear throughout the year.

2. Our class will make an ox-cart man quilt. Study the book carefully and decide what you will embroider on your square. Put your name and what you will embroider on the quilt sign-up sheet. There are many quilt books in the library center. You may find them helpful as you plan your square.

Portsmouth

- Is an ox a cow?
- Why was the needle an English needle? How did it get to this country?

Open-Ended Questions

- Why do you think people in Portsmouth needed to buy the items the ox-cart man sold? Do you think this family earned money only during the month of October? What will the family do with the coins the father had left over from his shopping?
- Why do you think the ox-cart man went alone on this trip? Where did he sleep at night? What did he have for food?
- What didn't the author tell us about family life on a farm during this time? What additional information do we want to know?
- How would you describe the relationships among the members of this family?
- Why do you think the author simply calls the man in the story the "ox-cart man"? Why do you think he chose not to name any of the family members? What were some common first names in those days?
- Why did the ox-cart man have to travel so far to sell the things his family made? Do you suppose people from Portsmouth ever came to the farm to buy food? Do you think the ox-cart man is the only farmer to sell things at Portsmouth Market?
- Why do you think Donald Hall wrote this story?
- Could this story happen today? What makes you say that?

Sample Activities for Strand One: Social Studies Content from Text and Illustrations

- Make a chart of the family's chores. Discuss with your group members which chores are done by one person and which are done by the family working together. Was that a good way of working? What do you think is the best chore? The most difficult?
- Study the picture of the market area in Portsmouth. What occupations were found in Portsmouth? Make a list of those jobs. Find through research

other important careers during this period. Add these jobs to your list. Circle those jobs that are no longer necessary in that community.

- Look at the opening illustrations in the book *Miss Rumphius* (Cooney 1982). Compare this illustration to the Portsmouth Market scene. Do you think these drawings could be of the same town? Be prepared to discuss your conclusions with the entire class.

- After looking at the illustrations in the books, make a list of examples of geographic features found in the region. Look at other books that show the physical and cultural features of this state to determine if the artist's illustrations are accurate. How do you think an illustrator could know what a place looked like more than one hundred years ago?

Sample Activities for Strand Two: Using Skills to Gather and Report Social Studies Data

- Design a one-year pictorial time line for this family. A manipulative time line would be an interesting way to do this. Students could pin colorful symbols to the time line with data on them. They could use small clothespins, gem clips, or binder clips to hold each symbol in place.

- Locate Portsmouth, New Hampshire, on a map. Find out how many miles per day a person could walk with an ox pulling a loaded cart. With this information, decide where the ox-cart man's farm would have been located. Could his farm have been in more than one place?

- Study a modern-day map of this area. If you retraced the route the ox-cart man took, through what cities or towns might you travel?

- Read carefully the description of what the ox-cart man saw on his trip to Portsmouth. Draw a pictorial map illustrating the route the ox-cart man took from his farm to Portsmouth.

- Investigate the following topics:
  a. How do people get sap from the maple tree? Do people still do this today? What must they do to process the sap? Draw a flowchart to show the steps in processing the sap.

  b. Read Rachel Field's *General Store* (1988). Compare that general store with the store the ox-cart man visited.

  c. Read other books from that time period and from that area of the country to compare the way each author and illustrator describes life in New England in the 1880s. For example, you might read *Hannah's Farm: The Seasons on an Early American Homestead* (McCurdy 1988).

Sample Activities for Strand Three: Creative Demonstration of Content Knowledge

- Plan a wax museum activity using scenes from the book. Invite another class to walk through the scenes in your museum while a narrator explains each scene (Gallagher and Lindquist 1988). Students plan each scene, decide who will be in each scene, and write the narrator's script. Gallagher and Lindquist (1988) suggest that students study *We the People* (Spier 1987) for examples of how many scenes can portray one idea.

- Write a diary from the perspective of one of the characters in the story. Include pages that might have appeared throughout a one-year period.

- The ox-cart man's daughter sends a letter by her father to a friend who still lives in Portsmouth. She invites the friend to come during the summer for a visit. She tells the friend some of the things they could do. Write that letter.

- Write a letter to a member of the family in the story. Invite that person to visit you. Explain what you would do if that person came for a visit. Make an agenda for what the person would see and do. What do you think the visitor will find amazing or surprising?

- Embroidering was an important skill during the nineteenth century. Have each student embroider a square about something from the story. Sew all the squares together to make a story quilt. Discuss the various types of quilts used during the nineteenth century.

The classroom teacher's responsibility does not end once students begin working with the folders. Teachers continue to interact with individual students and with small groups of learners. They continue to facilitate student learning through questions and suggestions, functioning as colearners with the students. Because groups of students will have diverse assignments, teachers will also need to plan ways for all students to benefit from the work of all groups.

Using literature folders to organize individual and group study of a topic in social studies is one strategy available to teachers. Like all strategies, you need to use it wisely and not overuse it. By using strategies such as literature folders, however, teachers can guide students' study of social studies topics while involving them with outstanding literature.

References

Cooney, Barbara. *Miss Rumphius*. New York: Penguin USA, Puffin Books, 1982.

dePaola, Tomie. *Charlie Needs a Cloak*. New York: Prentice-Hall, 1973.

Field, Rachel. *General Store*. Illustrated by Nancy Winslow Parker. New York: William Morrow and Co., Greenwillow Books, 1988.

Gallagher, Arlene, and Tarry Lindquist. "Children's Literature and Social Studies: Motivating the Young Learner." *Social Studies and the Young Learner* 2 (November/December 1988): 23–24.

Hall, Donald. *Ox-Cart Man*. New York: Penguin USA, Viking, 1979.

Hutchins, Pat. *Rosie's Walk*. New York: Macmillan Publishing Co., 1968.

Levstik, Linda. "Once Upon a Time Past: History in the Elementary Classroom." *Social Studies and the Young Learner* 2 (November/December 1989): 3–5.

_____. "Research Directions Mediating Content through Literary Texts." *Language Arts* 67 (December 1990): 848–53.

McCurdy, Michael. *Hannah's Farm: The Seasons on an Early American Homestead*. New York: Holiday House, 1988.

McGinley, William, and Daniel Madigan. "The Research 'Story': A Form for Integrating Reading, Writing and Learning." *Language Arts* 67(September 1990): 474–83.

Norton, Donna E. *The Impact of Literature-Based Reading*. New York: Macmillan Publishing Co., 1992.

Routman, Regie. *Transitions*. Portsmouth, N.H.: Heinemann Educational Books, 1988.

Savage, Tom V., and David G. Armstrong. *Effective Teaching in Elementary Social Studies*. New York: Macmillan Publishing Co., 1992.

Spier, Peter. *We the People: The Constitution of the United States*. New York: Doubleday, 1987.

VanSickle, Ronald L. "The Personal Relevance of the Social Studies." *Social Education* 55 (January 1990): 23–27, 59.

Zarrillo, James. "History and Library Books." *Social Studies and the Young Learner* 2 (November/December 1989): 17–18.

Chapter Twelve

People Who Take Risks: A Focus Unit

Jacqueline A. Abbott

Some people have an insatiable curiosity—a curiosity about the unknown, the new, the unusual. Few people allow that curiosity to carry them to new places, new sounds, new sights, and to different ways of looking at the world. Those who do are the risk takers—the bold and daring people who put fear aside and conquer new worlds, who ignore the doubters and make a thing of beauty cast in a different form.

This generation of students admires sports personalities, rock stars, and fantasy heroes from the land of television and pulp books. They accomplish the impossible instantly. All too quickly, students realize that opportunities for them to reach the apex of a career in basketball or with a popular music group are one in several million. So where are the role models for these citizens of the twenty-first century?

Young citizens require heroes that are ordinary people—ordinary in every way except for a quality that separates them from the crowd. The quality is that of a risk taker. Risk takers are defined here as those people who have dreams, ideas, and goals and who set about to achieve those goals. Espousing an idea that is brand new and will solve a problem is taking a risk. Creating a device that will save lives in the future is taking a risk. Exploring new places from a different perspective is taking risk. Through reading about risk takers, identifying with them, and practicing taking risks themselves, students learn that dreaming and goal setting are desirable.

The purpose of this paper is to show students that risk taking is desirable and that risk takers are ordinary human beings like themselves. Risk takers invent, discover, create, lead, serve, and may even become famous. This paper will focus on six such people whose stories are told in six recent biographies—all cited as National Council for the Social Studies-Children's Book Council Notable Trade Books in the Field of Social Studies.

The risk-taking theme correlates with three scope-and-sequence models identified by the NCSS Ad Hoc Committee on Scope and Sequence (NCSS 1989). This unit specifically addresses three criteria:
1. building self-esteem;
2. incorporating thinking skills and interpersonal skills at all levels; and
3. promoting the transfer of knowledge and skills to life.

The research literature supports the benefits of using literature to teach social studies content. The fine books presented here are representative of the many well-researched and well-presented books available to students. Teachers can, of course, use other books and activities that relate to specific social studies curriculum in place of those used here. Teachers can also apply this model—an example of the focus unit approach (Moss 1984)—to other topics using books that feature people who solved problems for the benefit of humanity and those who developed and shared a talent to make the world a better place.

Literature Goals
- Develop literary taste.
- Increase enjoyment of literature.
- Build communication skills.

Duration of the Unit
Five to six weeks.

Grade Level
6th, 7th, and 8th.

Books Used
Ferris, Jeri. *Arctic Explorer: The Story of Matthew Henson*. Illustrated with photographs. New York: Carolrhoda Books, 1989. "An honest, first-rate biography of Matthew Henson, the black explorer, who accompanied Robert Peary on six expe-

From *Arctic Explorer: The Story of Matthew Henson*, © 1989 Jeri Ferris, reprinted by permission of Carolrhoda Books.

From *Julia Morgan: Architect of Dreams*, © 1990 Ginger Wadsworth, reprinted by permission of Lerner Publications Company.

ditions to the North Pole" ("Notable" 1990).

Fisher, Leonard Everett. *Prince Henry the Navigator.* Illustrated in black and white by the author. New York: Macmillan Publishing Co., 1990. "A boldly illustrated, straightforward biography of Portugal's Prince Henry (1394–1460) [that] emphasizes contributions to navigation [including] the founding of the first maritime institute, improvements in the circular astrolabe, the triangular quadrant and the compass, and the invention of a new type of vessel. It includes a chronology of the Iberian Peninsula (711–1498), a map, and an afterword that traces a direct line to Columbus' expeditions" ("Notable" 1991).

Hook, Jason. *The Voyages of Captain Cook.* Illustrated by Richard Hook. New York: Franklin Watts, 1990. Captain Cook's explorations and achievements are featured in this chapter book, using a two-page spread with paintings from original sources. The varied illustrations supply the reader with much additional information. A manage-

able book for upper elementary school students.

Levinson, Nancy Smiley. *Christopher Columbus: Voyager to the Unknown.* Illustrated with black-and-white prints and maps. New York: Penguin USA, Lodestar, 1990. "A straightforward, detailed description of Columbus' four voyages and the relationships he and his men established with Native Americans emphasizes the many perspectives from which a historian can consider Columbus' story. Includes a chronology of events, listing of crew members, and letters of authorization in a handsome format" ("Notable" 1991).

Roth, Susan L. *Marco Polo.* New York: Doubleday, 1991. This is a handsome and informative representation of the log of Marco Polo as he travels to and from China. The twelfth-century-style illustrations enhance the diary format, lending a feeling of authenticity. Excitement takes the reader along on the travels. It is simple and elegant.

Wadsworth, Ginger. *Julia Morgan: Architect of*

Dreams. Illustrated with color and black-and-white photographs and diagrams. New York: Lerner Publications Co., 1990. "A biography of Julia Morgan, female pioneer in the field of architecture, provides insights into the personal and professional life of the designer of [more than seven hundred] buildings, including Hearst Castle. Includes a directory of buildings by the architect" ("Notable" 1991).

Lesson 1
Objectives
- Students will identify people they admire and list qualities that person possesses.
- Students will be able to tell what they know about each of six risk takers identified by the teacher.
- Students will select a book of their choice and read about one risk taker.

Materials
Several copies of the six books listed.

Procedure
1. Brainstorm a list of people that students admire, listing the names on the chalkboard. Ask what it is about these individuals that students admire and list the responses. What are some qualities that seem to stand out on the list?

2. Paraphrase or read the following: "I've selected some books that are biographies about people that I believe fit our description of risk takers and possibly the kind of people you say you admire." Hold up each book and offer students an opportunity to identify the person in the biography and share information they know about that person.

3. Suggest that students take time to look at the books and eventually select one to read. "We will use these books to meet people who have taken risks in the past and develop a more complete understanding of what made them do what they did. We will find other people in stories, perhaps from our own time, that have similar qualities."

4. Students will read their chosen book independently or with a partner and be asked to share interesting information they discover, especially evidence of risk taking.

Lessons 2 to 5
Objectives
- Students will identify places visited by Marco Polo after hearing the book read aloud.
- Students will role-play selected entries in Marco Polo's diary and be able to identify qualities that he possessed and experience how he might have felt.
- Students will write diary entries for the risk taker about whom they have been reading.

Materials
Copies of the six books, writing materials, paper cut and put together as a diary or journal for each student, and props for role-play (e.g., hats, a heavy jacket, navigational instruments, drafting paper, and pens).

Procedure
1. Read diary entries from *Marco Polo* aloud to the class. Stop frequently and allow student to comment on places and adventures Polo experienced.
- Which of these places do you know about?
- Could you find them on a map?
- Do you think they still have the same name?
- Is reading from a diary a good way to learn about a person? How do you know?
- Besides the places Polo visited and the things he saw, what else do we know about him?
- Was Marco Polo a risk taker in your opinion?
- What made him so?

2. Provide students with a hat and robe for Marco Polo and invite them to role-play a scene from his diary. Encourage several students to work with different scenes.
- How did it feel to be Marco Polo?
- What qualities were you able to feel while you were portraying him?
- Did you feel like a risk taker?

3. Provide props that represent the other five people, e.g., a winter parka for Matthew Henson, navigation instruments for Prince Henry, Columbus, and Captain Cook, and drafting paper and pens for Julia Morgan. Invite students to role-play scenes from the books they have been reading and repeat the

same questions found above.

4. The author of *Marco Polo* created a diary from Polo's own writing and from what other people wrote about him. Ask students to create a diary for the risk taker they have read about, selecting events that could be of interest to other readers and try to make the entries tell the reader ways that person is a risk taker. Provide students opportunities to write several entries over time and write the finished copy in a diary. You can preserve these.

Lessons 6 to 17

Objectives

- Students will examine the attitudes and actions of Columbus, Prince Henry, and Captain Cook that were hurtful and cruel to some people and contrast these negative actions and attitudes with their accomplishments.
- Using the "Know, Want to Know, Learn" stragegy (Ogle 1989), students will identify what they know about Prince Henry the Navigator, what they would like to know, and information they have learned from the book.
- Students will conduct a roundtable discussion about Columbus and involve other students in relating information about him, his actions, and his accomplishments.
- In small groups, students will tell the story of Captain Cook and ask other students to respond to questions about Cook's actions and accomplishments.
- Students will organize information on a chart about the three risk takers and be able to make comparisons and generalizations.

Materials

The books *Prince Henry the Navigator, Christopher Columbus: Voyager to the Unknown,* and *The Voyages of Captain Cook.*

Procedure

1. Show the cover of the book *Prince Henry the Navigator* and ask students what they know about this man. What might the word *navigator* mean? Develop a chart with the students, encouraging them to tell first what they know about Prince Henry, then what they would like to know, and finally what they learned from the story. Read the story aloud. Complete the last part of the chart with the class. Add more questions to the want-to-know list. Seek other books and references for answers to these questions.

2. Note the reference in the book to the new ships Henry requested to replace the clumsy and slow ships of the time with the caravel, a faster, wider, longer ship. With increased range and speed, the Portuguese ships traveled farther and also found goods, such as gold, that were more interesting than those of other countries. Then the slave trade began. Prince Henry, according to Fisher, ignored the kidnapping of Africans and the poor treatment they received. Discuss the long-term effects of the beginnings of the slave trade using the following questions.

- Can you think of any reasons that the improvement of the astrolabe, the quadrant, the compass, and the development of the caravel by Prince Henry led to the beginning of the slave trade?
- What do you know about the treatment of Africans on slave ships and later at the hands of slave owners?
- Was this practice right then? Would this practice be right today?
- What would you tell Prince Henry about the long-term effects of his improvements on navigation if you could talk to him today?

3. Ask students who have read the book *Christopher Columbus: Voyager to the Unknown* to discuss information they learned about Columbus. Emphasize the following points:

- Columbus lived at the same time as Prince Henry.
- Columbus was curious about a route to the riches of China and the Far East that was shorter than that reported by Marco Polo.
- Columbus made four voyages. On each one he explored different places, had many adventures, and met different people.
- Columbus's treatment of people that he met was not always kind or humane.
- Columbus struggled his entire life to get people in

power to believe him.
* Columbus was a risk taker.

4. Focus on Columbus's treatment of Native Americans through discussion. Levinson includes some recent research findings about that treatment. Pose questions similar to those posed about Prince Henry.

5. Ask students who have read *The Voyages of Captain Cook* to share the book with other class members by telling the story in small groups. Encourage the storytellers to ask two questions of their group:
* In what ways was Captain Cook a risk taker?
* How did Captain Cook treat the people he met in his travels?

6. As a whole-class activity, develop a chart comparing and contrasting the three men. Include accomplishments, treatment of people, evidence of risk taking, and other topics that students identify. Following the collection of data, make generalizations about the three risk takers by making statements about them. Encourage students to gather additional information by reading other books that may contain new information or a different viewpoint.

Lessons 18 to 25
Objectives
* Students will be able to discuss Julia Morgan and relate her impossible dream by writing their own impossible dream with a solution for making that dream come true.
* Students will be able to discuss Matthew Henson in relation to Robert Peary and select the man they would prefer to emulate.
* Students will analyze the original definition of *risk taker* and redefine the term in light of new information brought about through this study.
* Students will read about two present-day risk takers and compose a series of letters between the two individuals that describe their accomplishments and their qualities.
* Students will interview an individual from their local environment whom they consider a risk taker and write a biographical sketch that demonstrates risk-taking qualities.

* Students will write an autobiography that describes risk-taking qualities they possess.

Materials
The books *Julia Morgan: Architect of Dreams* and *Arctic Explorer: The Story of Matthew Henson,* and a variety of biographies featuring risk takers who have lived in the past decade.

Procedure
1. Ask students if they have heard these words before: "My buildings will be my legacy....They will speak for themselves long after I'm gone." Those students who have chosen to read *Julia Morgan* will be able to identify her. Rely on these students to summarize Julia Morgan's accomplishments, important aspects of her life, and her qualities. Pose several questions:
* Is it difficult to imagine how in the late 1800s certain fields of endeavor were closed to women?
* Have there been other girls and women who dreamed of being an architect or an engineer or a doctor but whose dreams were out of the question or forbidden?
* What special qualities has the author presented to the reader about Morgan that could explain how she dreamed and how her dreams came true? How did fulfilling her own dreams inspire other women?

2. Ask students to write down one of their dreams that seems impossible and then explain why they think it is unachievable. Ask them to conclude with ideas that could make the dream come true. Encourage students to illustrate their stories.

3. Discuss excerpts from *Arctic Explorer: The Story of Matthew Henson* that recall his skills in language, survival, navigation, building igloos, and carpentry. Encourage students who have read this book to include information about the book in a chart:
* What we know about Peary.
* What we know about Henson.
* What we know about the expeditions.
* Other information.

Discuss the risk takers in this book. Contrast the qualities of Peary and Henson. With whom would you prefer to explore? Who would you prefer to be like? Give reasons.

4. Having read about six risk takers from different historical periods, return to the original definition and see if it is true now in light of new knowledge. Add to the definition if the class believes it is necessary.

5. Encourage students to identify contemporary risk takers. An initial brainstorming list might include Mikhail Gorbachev, Sally Ride, Nelson Mandela, Magic Johnson, Benazir Bhutto, Christa McAuliffe, Diane Fossey, Jesse Jackson, Benjamin Cohen and Jerry Greenfield (the founders of Ben and Jerry's Ice Cream), Frederick Smith (the founder of Federal Express), and Ray Kroc (the founder of McDonald's). Provide books that feature risk takers. Ask students to read about two of these people and write a series of three or four letters between the individuals that help us to understand them, what motivates them, and why they take risks.

6. Ask students to identify a person they know from their town, school, neighborhood, or family who is a risk taker. Prepare a set of questions and interview this person. Prepare a biographical sketch of your risk taker and be ready to present it to the class in the format of your choice (e.g., a written biography, an oral biography, a monologue, a role-play, or a poem).

7. Are you a risk taker? Ask students to describe themselves in writing in ways that will bring out qualities that make them risk takers. Self-portraits are encouraged as part of this final assignment.

References

Ferris, Jeri. *Arctic Explorer: The Story of Matthew Henson.* Minneapolis, Minn.: Carolrhoda Books, 1989.

Fisher, Leonard Everett. *Prince Henry the Navigator.* New York: Macmillan Publishing Co., 1990.

Hook, Jason. *The Voyages of Captain Cook.* Illustrated by Richard Hook. New York: Franklin Watts, 1990.

Levinson, Nancy Smiley. *Christopher Columbus: Voyager to the Unknown.* New York: Penguin USA, Lodestar Books, 1990.

Moss, Joy S. *Focus Units in Literature: A Handbook for Elementary School Teachers.* Urbana, Ill.: National Council of Teachers of English, 1984.

National Council for the Social Studies. "Report of the Ad Hoc Committee on Scope and Sequence." *Social Education* 53 (October 1989): 375–76.

"Notable 1989 Children's Trade Books in the Field of Social Studies." *Social Education* 54 (April/May 1990): 219–26.

"Notable 1990 Children's Trade Books in the Field of Social Studies." *Social Education* 55 (April/May 1991): 253–60.

Ogle, Donna M. "The Know, Want to Know, Learn Strategy." In *Children's Comprehension of Text: Research into Practice*, edited by K. Denise Muth, 205–23. Newark, Del.: International Reading Association, 1989.

Notes

Notes